The Universe

TIME LIFE   Student Library

The Universe

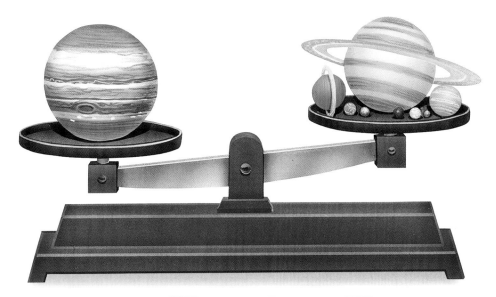

Time-Life Books

Table of Contents

The Universe

Twinkle, Twinkle Many Stars

The universe is huge beyond imagining. Every night, a tiny portion of it is revealed to us in the starry sky overhead. Mixed in among the **stars** are **planets, moons,** star clusters, **nebulae,** and **galaxies.** Once in a while we are treated to the glowing tail of a passing **comet** or the fleeting streak of a **meteor.** In this picture, the white glow of a star cluster is visible through the tree branches, and what appears to be a fluffy pink cloud *(centre)* is in fact a cloud made up entirely of stars that lies in front of the centre of our galaxy, the Milky Way.

What Is the Universe?

The universe is all the **matter, energy,** and space that exist. It includes everything from the crumbs on your kitchen floor to the Sun, the **planets,** all the **stars** and **galaxies,** the **dust** and **gas** between the stars, and the light that travels through space. The universe is all of these things together. The word 'universe' comes from the Latin phrase meaning 'turning as one'.

Although it is hard to tell from where we stand, the universe has a structure. Planets **orbit** stars. Stars, billions of them, clump together into galaxies. There are about 100 billion galaxies altogether in the universe. Most galaxies are found in groups called clusters. Clusters, in turn, usually form even larger groups, called superclusters. Finally, superclusters cling to one another in even more enormous structures that look like walls or sheets of galaxies. These unimaginably huge groupings are the largest features of the universe.

Beautiful as gems on black velvet, hundreds of galaxies glow in this image from the Hubble Space Telescope. This 'deep field' picture was made by piecing together 276 photographs taken of a tiny area of the sky—a portion as small as a grain of sand held at arm's length. The picture is 'deep' because it shows galaxies billions of **light-years** away.

Fast FACTS

The Scale of the Universe

Earth 12,756 km (7,926 miles) across

Sun 1,392,000 km (864,900 miles) across

Earth's Orbit About 300 million km (186 million miles) across

Pluto's Orbit About 12 billion km (7 billion miles) across

Milky Way Galaxy 100,000 light-years across

Local Group 6 million light-years across

Local Supercluster 80 million light-years across

Observable Universe 26 to 30 billion light-years across

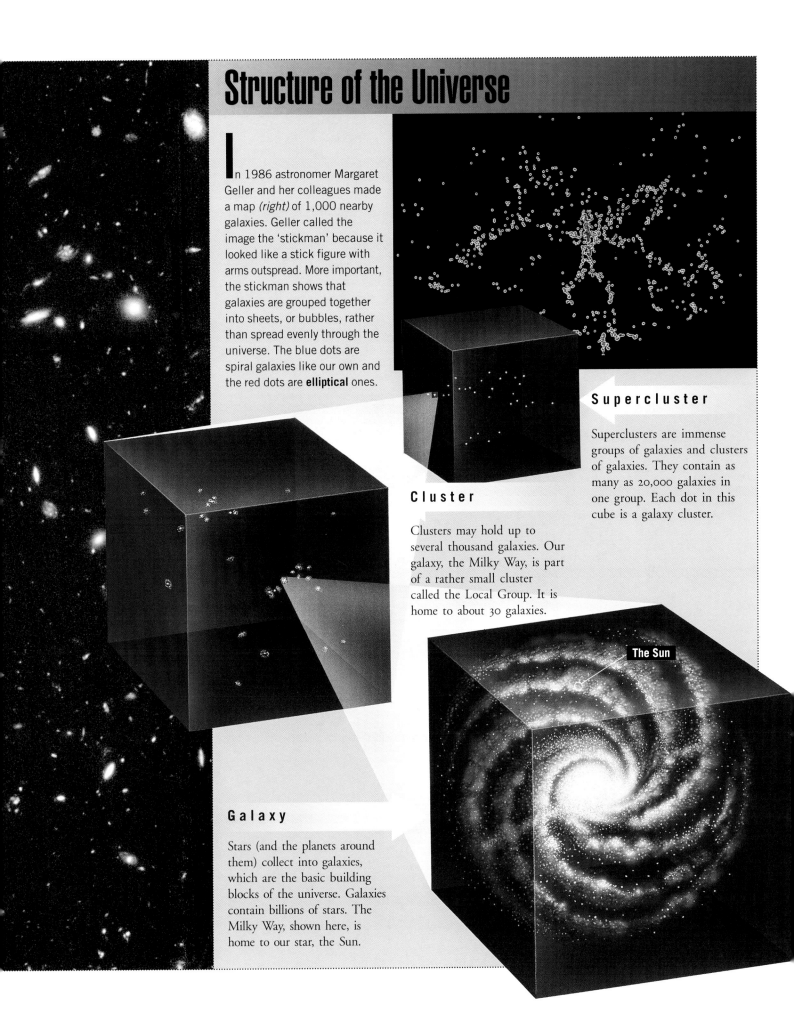

Structure of the Universe

In 1986 astronomer Margaret Geller and her colleagues made a map *(right)* of 1,000 nearby galaxies. Geller called the image the 'stickman' because it looked like a stick figure with arms outspread. More important, the stickman shows that galaxies are grouped together into sheets, or bubbles, rather than spread evenly through the universe. The blue dots are spiral galaxies like our own and the red dots are **elliptical** ones.

Supercluster

Superclusters are immense groups of galaxies and clusters of galaxies. They contain as many as 20,000 galaxies in one group. Each dot in this cube is a galaxy cluster.

Cluster

Clusters may hold up to several thousand galaxies. Our galaxy, the Milky Way, is part of a rather small cluster called the Local Group. It is home to about 30 galaxies.

The Sun

Galaxy

Stars (and the planets around them) collect into galaxies, which are the basic building blocks of the universe. Galaxies contain billions of stars. The Milky Way, shown here, is home to our star, the Sun.

How Big Is the Universe?

Ancient scientists believed that the Earth was the centre of the universe and that the Sun, **stars,** and **planets** circled it nearby. Not until the 20th century, when we built some powerful telescopes, did we learn that our Sun was just one modest star among billions of **galaxies** in the deep reaches of space. Now astronomers want to know just how far away those galaxies are.

When we look at distant stars or galaxies, we are looking back in time. Light from a galaxy 1 billion **light-years** away has been travelling one billion years to reach us. That means that if the universe is 13 to 15 billion years old, the edge of the observable universe is about 13 to 15 billion light-years away. In 1998, the Keck II telescope in Hawaii (one of the most powerful in the world) picked up light from a galaxy more than 12 billion light-years away. That light had been travelling for a long, long time! If scientists are right about the age of the universe, then the observable universe may extend past that for another 1 to 3 billion light-years.

What's a Light-year?

Because normal units of measurement are simply too small to use for the enormous distances between stars, astronomers use the term 'light-years'. Light makes a good cosmic yardstick because it always travels at the same speed—299,000 km (186,000 miles) per second. A light-year is the distance light travels in one year. It is equal to about 10 trillion km (6 trillion miles).

How Long?

A Trip to the Nearest Star

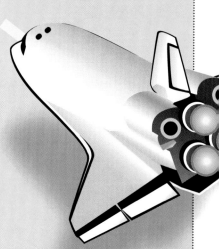

Forget about travelling across the universe. How long would it take to reach the star closest to our Sun? Proxima Centauri, our nearest stellar neighbour, is 4.3 light-years away. That's about 43 trillion km (27 trillion miles). Riding in the space shuttle, rocketing along at 27,000 km (17,000 miles) per hour, it would take us 170,000 years to reach the star. Better pack a lot of snacks!

People

It was American Astronomer Henrietta Swan Leavitt, who discovered a way to find out a star's distance from Earth. In 1908, Leavitt was working in the Harvard College Observatory. She noticed that a certain kind of star, called a Cepheid variable, would grow dim and bright and dim again in a regular pattern. The timing of this pattern was directly related to the star's true brightness. Astronomers were able to compare the true brightness of these stars with their **apparent brightness** as seen through telescopes on Earth. This told them how far away the stars were. Leavitt's discovery paved the way for the discovery of galaxies.

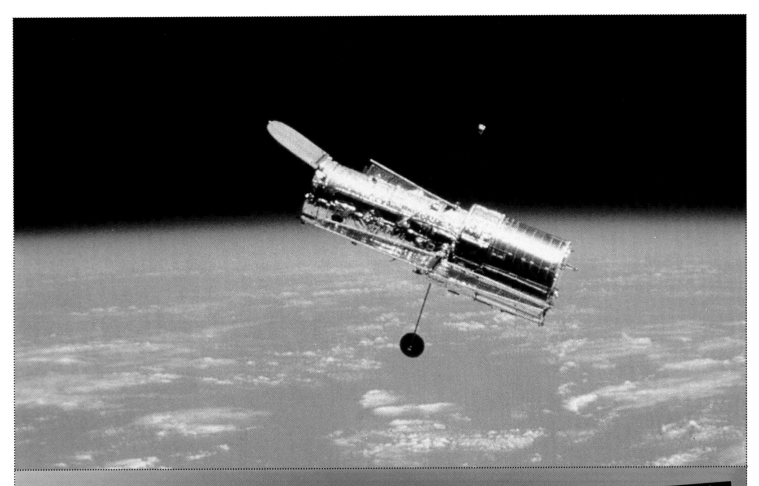

Edwin Hubble

Edwin Hubble *(below)*, a tall athletic American, studied law and Spanish before deciding to become an astronomer in 1914. He went on to make two of the most important discoveries of modern science.

Until Hubble's time, scientists believed that our galaxy, the Milky Way, was the entire universe. But when Hubble studied the distances to stars in what was then known as the Andromeda Nebula *(right)*, he discovered that they were far outside the edges of the Milky Way. The Andromeda Nebula was another galaxy! (Today it has been measured at about 2.3 million light-years away.)

Hubble later found that the sky was full of galaxies, and they were moving away from one another. This told scientists that the universe is expanding. The Hubble Space Telescope *(above)* is named in his honour.

The Big Bang

When astronomers realized that the universe was expanding, they also realized that in the past it must have been smaller than it is now. In fact, about 13 to 15 billion years ago—which is about the time most scientists believe the universe began—the entire universe was squashed into a tremendously dense, unbelievably hot speck. This infant universe was too hot and full of **energy** to stay small. In a flash, it expanded outward. We call this instant of cosmic birth the **Big Bang.**

The Big Bang was not like an explosion. **Matter** and energy did not go flying out into space. There was no space outside of the Big Bang. There wasn't even any time before the Big Bang. Time started when the universe began to expand. Gradually, the intensely hot energy soup of the early universe began to cool down. After millions of years, **gas, stars,** and **galaxies** were formed. After about 8 to 10 billion years, our **solar system** and our Earth appeared. So in universal time, we've only just arrived!

Try it!

Blow Up the Universe

To understand the expanding universe, pick up a deflated balloon and a marker. Draw galaxies on the balloon. Then blow it up. Can you see how all the galaxies move away from all the other galaxies on the expanding balloon? In this way, galaxies move apart in the expanding fabric of space.

From Energy to Galaxies

1. Pure energy
In the first fraction of a second after the Big Bang, the universe has expanded to the size of a grapefruit. It is made of pure, hot energy.

2. Particles
At one second, the universe is about the size of our solar system. It is one million times hotter than the centre of the Sun. The tiny particles— **protons, electrons,** and **neutrons**—that make up **atoms** have been formed.

3. Nuclei
After five minutes, the cooling universe looks like a dense fog. Protons and neutrons have joined to create the first centres (nuclei) of the first atoms—deuterium and helium.

4. Atoms
Electrons join protons and neutrons to form hydrogen atoms. The fog clears and light shines through the universe.

5. Stars
Clouds of hydrogen and helium gas cool and form protogalaxies (baby galaxies). Within these protogalaxies, the first stars appear.

6. Galaxies
Groups of stars come together to make small galaxies. Over time the galaxies merge to form the larger galaxies we see today.

The Big Bang	One second	Five minutes
1	2	3

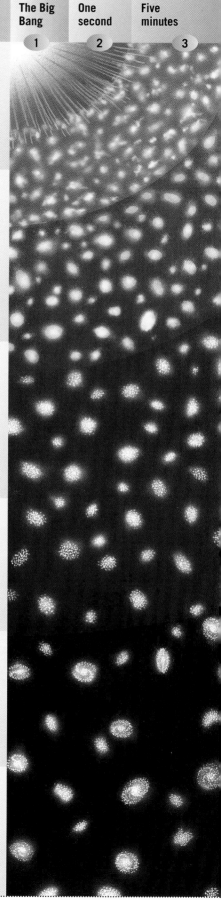

How **Fast?**

When you stand on your lawn and look up at the stars, they don't seem to be going anywhere very fast. But think of this: astronomer Hyron Spinrad says that in the time it takes you to read this paragraph, typical distant galaxy clusters have moved apart by 1.6 million km (1 million miles). That's how fast the universe is expanding!

The **Big Bang** is a thrilling idea, but is it true? How can we really know what happened 13 to 15 billion years ago?

Even though the Big Bang took place so long ago, it left three major clues. The first is the motion of the still-expanding universe. By studying the light from distant **galaxies,** astronomers can tell that they are all moving away from one another. The second clue is the large amount of helium in the **cosmos.** The theory of the Big Bang predicted that early particles would form into helium and hydrogen **gas,** with 1 helium **atom** for every 12 hydrogen atoms. In 1995, a telescope on the space shuttle measured these interstellar gases. The result: 1 helium atom for every 12 hydrogen atoms.

The third clue is something called cosmic background **radiation.** The radiation left over from the birth of the universe has cooled down, but it is still out there, and scientific instruments have found it.

Cosmic Radiation

The discovery of cosmic background radiation is a story of smart guys, luck, and pigeon droppings.

By the 1940s, some astronomers were predicting that radiation from the Big Bang should still be out there in space. It would be very difficult to find but still detectable.

In 1964, a group of astronomers at Princeton University, in the USA—including Dave Wilkinson *(right)*—decided to build an antenna to search for this radiation. But while they were building it, they were beaten to it. Close by, at Bell Telephone Laboratories, radio astronomers Arno Penzias *(above, right)* and Robert Wilson *(above, left)* were having trouble with an annoying hum in an antenna they had built. For a while they thought it was caused by pigeon droppings on the surface. But when they told the Princeton group that the temperature of whatever was making this weird hum was measured at 3.5°K—just above **absolute zero** (-273°C, -459°F) —the Princeton astronomers knew that the Bell Labs scientists had discovered the leftover radiation from the Big Bang. Penzias and Wilson went on to win the Nobel prize.

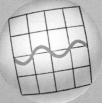

How do we Know?

Redshift

We know that other galaxies are moving away from ours because of an effect called 'redshift'. The light from **stars** can be broken down into a **spectrum** *(page 16)*, a rainbow that ranges from red to violet. Light moves in waves, and each colour has its own **wavelength**—red waves are long and violet waves are short. Light from distant galaxies shows a change in its spectrum. Its waves stretch, or 'shift' toward the red end of the spectrum. This happens because space is expanding, carrying galaxies away from us.

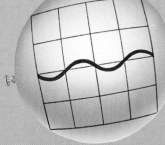

Infant Universe

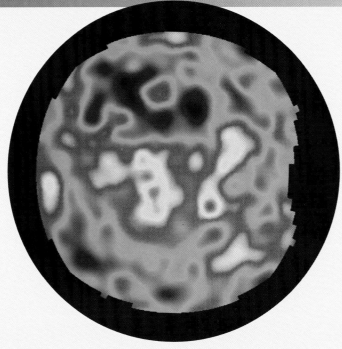

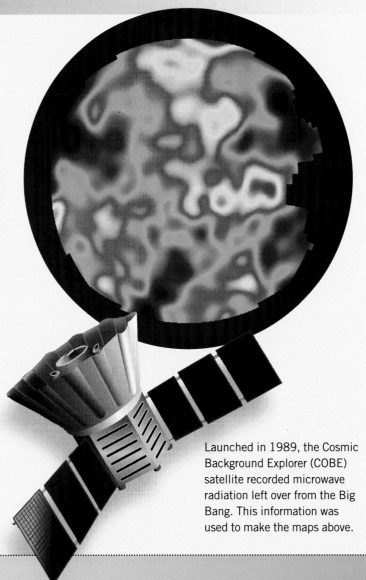

The two glowing circles above are baby pictures—images of the universe when it was only 300,000 years old. That was the age when light first shone freely through space. Now **satellites** can find the dim remains of that radiation and map it. On the left is the universe above our galaxy; on the right, the universe below. The colours, assigned by computer, show tiny differences in temperature between regions. Red is the hottest, violet the coldest. These differences show that the early universe was not smooth; it was kind of lumpy. It had emptier (blue) and denser (red) regions that would later form into galaxies.

Launched in 1989, the Cosmic Background Explorer (COBE) satellite recorded microwave radiation left over from the Big Bang. This information was used to make the maps above.

How Will the Universe End?

Astronomers have two major theories about how the universe will end. Which one of them turns out to be correct depends on how much **mass**—or stuff— the universe contains. If the cosmos has less than a certain amount of mass, it is 'open', and will keep expanding until all stars burn out. As it expands, it will get colder and colder, ending in a very frigid death. If it has more mass, then it is 'closed'. When it reaches a certain size, it will stop expanding and start to contract, collapsing like a reverse Big Bang into what scientists call the 'Big Crunch'. In this scenario, the universe will get hotter and hotter as all its **matter** is crunched into an unimaginably tiny space.

Open

Closed

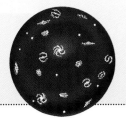

What Is Light?

How do we learn about **planets** and **stars**—objects so far away we can't visit them or touch them? We learn by observing their light. Light can tell us an amazing amount of information.

By light, we mean not just the **visible light** that our eyes can see, but the whole family that it belongs to—all forms of **electromagnetic radiation.** Radiation is the way that **energy** moves through space. Visible light and other kinds of electromagnetic radiation behave as though they are waves, rippling through space at unimaginably fast speeds. Some waves up to several metres long have been observed. Others are microscopically short. All these waves, from short to long, can be thought of as existing side by side on an **electromagnetic spectrum** *(below).*

Instruments today can capture all kinds of radiation. Each kind tells astronomers different things about the object that it came from. Cold **gas** clouds give off invisible infrared waves. Matter swirling around black holes blasts out intense x-rays—signals of violent activity. Tiny stars called **pulsars** pump out radio waves. Light can tell us what an object is made of, how hot it is, how fast it is moving, and if it is moving toward us or away from us.

Let's Compare

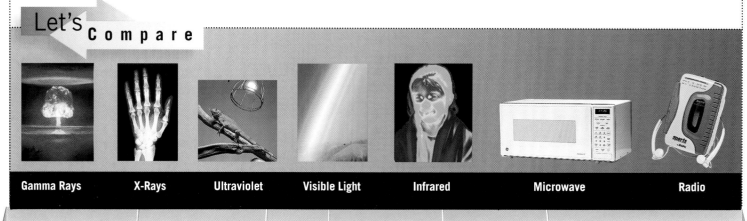

| Gamma Rays | X-Rays | Ultraviolet | Visible Light | Infrared | Microwave | Radio |

Short wavelengths   Long wavelengths

Electromagnetic Wavelengths

In a way, the visible light that shines on your book and the microwaves that cook your food are the same thing. They're both forms of electromagnetic radiation. In empty space, all forms of electromagnetic energy zoom along at the same speed—the speed of light, 299,000 km (186,000 miles) per second. All electromagnetic waves can be arranged on a spectrum *(above),* a kind of graph that ranks them from the shortest gamma rays to the longest radio waves. Visible light, what our eyes see, is in the middle. It has waves just a fraction of a centimetre long. Scientists often talk about shorter **wavelengths** as being at the 'blue' end of the spectrum and longer wavelengths as being at the 'red' end.

The Sun's Many Faces

Radio

Bright spots on a blue disk show active areas in the outer layers of the Sun's **atmosphere.** Particle collisions in these regions produce radio waves.

Everything can give off radiation. Objects from **atoms** to icebergs send out waves that are spread across part of the electromagnetic spectrum *(previous page)*. With the right instruments, scientists can study that radiation at each wavelength. Every kind of wave can tell them something new.

The Sun is a big, hot example of this. It gives off most of its radiation in the visible-light range of the spectrum. This is obvious to us every day when the Sun rises over the horizon. But the Sun radiates at many other wavelengths as well, some invisible to our senses but detectable to science. Each kind of radiation can be turned into a picture *(left)* that tells us something different about the Sun.

Visible

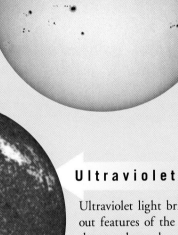

The surface of the Sun, in visible light, is called the photosphere. This image shows **sunspots** as dark specks.

Ultraviolet

Ultraviolet light brings out features of the chromosphere, the solar atmosphere closest to the Sun's surface. Bright spots are active regions.

X-Rays

The **corona,** the uppermost region of the Sun, contains areas so hot that they give off x-rays. An x-ray image reveals the violent, stormy nature of this highest layer.

Imagine That!

Seeing with Radio Eyes

When you look at the night sky, your eyes see the visible light given off by the stars. But if you could see radio waves instead, the sky would look like it does here. Shown above a visible-light image of the National Radio Astronomy Observatory in the USA is the 'radio sky'. The Milky Way extends from lower left to upper right. Bright spots are radio galaxies or **quasars**—bright centres of extremely distant galaxies.

What Is Gravity?

Gravity shapes the universe. It is a force that acts on all objects so that they are attracted to one another. **Gravity** pulls a thrown cricket ball toward the ground. It keeps the stars in our **galaxy** together.

The great English scientist Isaac Newton was the first person to describe gravity clearly. In 1664, he had to leave his studies as a university student in Cambridge, because the plague had sprung up there. While at home, mulling over such basic problems as the nature of light and the **orbit** of the planets, he figured out the basic law of gravity. He came to understand that every **mass**—every amount of **matter**—attracted every other mass. The strength of the attraction depended on the total amount of mass and the distance between the masses.

Newton's law of gravity still gives an excellent description of the way objects behave in ordinary circumstances.

However, the 20th-century physicist Albert Einstein took theories of gravity one giant step further. In 1915, he wrote that space and time are really part of the same fabric. Massive objects, such as **stars,** curve the space-time around them. This curve is gravity.

Isaac Newton figured out that gravity was a force that affected all objects.

A famous, but unproved, story about Isaac Newton says that the young scientist started wondering about gravity when he saw an apple fall from a tree. Why, he pondered, didn't the Moon also fall?

Albert Einstein understood that gravity was the effect of curved space-time.

Zero Gravity

Why are astronauts—such as Mae Jemison *(right)*, aboard the space shuttle in 1992—weightless? Have they somehow escaped gravity?

Floating astronauts are actually in 'free fall'. Gravity-wise, a spaceship orbiting the Earth is constantly falling. At the same time, its forward motion pulls it away from the **planet.** These two forces keep the ship in orbit—and its astronauts off the deck.

Warped Space

Big, massive objects, such as the Sun, pull the surface of space-time into a deep 'gravity well'. Smaller objects, such as the nearby planet Mercury, create shallower wells.

Einstein's theories forced astronomers to look at space in an entirely new way. They had to picture space as a vast stretchy fabric. Massive objects pull on the fabric, creating 'dents' called gravity wells in its surface. The Sun would create a big sag in the space-time fabric. A little **asteroid** would hardly mark it. Now picture a ray of light travelling along the surface of the space-time fabric. As it comes near the Sun's gravity well, it follows the curved surface of the space around the Sun. This causes it to take a tiny bit longer to reach Earth than if it follows a straight line. Observations of starlight passing near the Sun have shown this to be true—one of the many proofs of Einstein's work.

Einstein's Cross

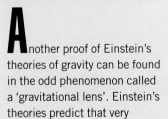

Another proof of Einstein's theories of gravity can be found in the odd phenomenon called a 'gravitational lens'. Einstein's theories predict that very massive objects, such as stars or galaxies, will bend the light that passes by them. Sometimes the light gets split around both sides of the massive object and reappears on the other side as two images *(below)*. In rare cases, known as an Einstein cross *(left)*, the light might split four ways around the object, creating four images of the same object to telescopes back on Earth. The cross is made up of four images of the same **quasar** (a centre of a very bright galaxy) around an image of a very big galaxy. The light from the quasar is being bent by the big galaxy.

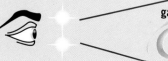

galaxy   quasar

Would **You** *Believe?*

Gravity as a Lens

Imagine standing outside on the grass looking at the building in the picture. Suddenly, a black hole with the mass of Saturn forms between you and the building. The black hole would serve as a gravitational lens. Light from the building would warp around the black hole, causing it to split into the two twisted images shown here (one upside down and one right side up).

What Is Matter?

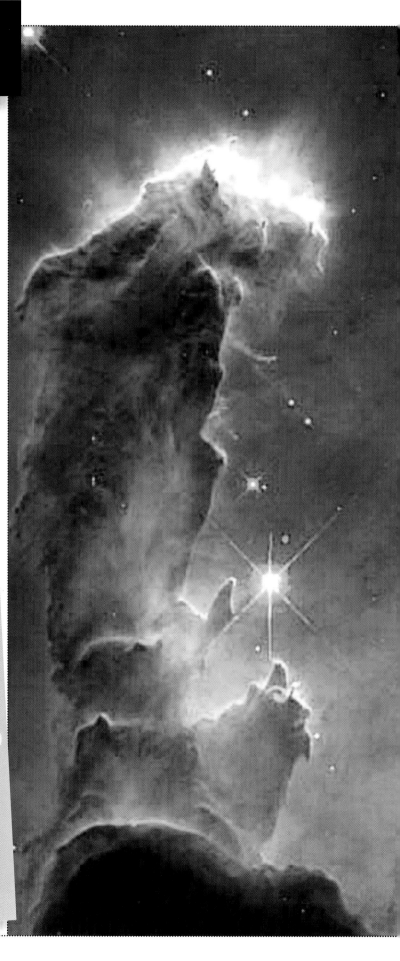

Matter is the stuff that any physical object is made of. The basic unit of **matter,** its tiny building block, is the **atom.** Atoms are so small that 10 million of them could fit between any two words in this sentence.

Different kinds of atoms make up the about 90 naturally occurring **elements** on Earth. All of them were formed in space. Hydrogen and most helium appeared in the **Big Bang** *(pages* 12-13*).* **Stars** gave birth to the rest. The tremendous heat inside a star fuses simple atoms together to form more complex ones. Three helium atoms combine into one carbon atom. Two carbon atoms become magnesium.

Heavier elements come from the death of big stars. As it burns up its fuel, a huge star will make these elements in its **core,** growing hotter until it explodes in a blinding **supernova.** Elements such as silicon and iron then fly out into space. In the centuries to follow, they gradually clump together, forming rocks, **planets**—and you.

What's an Atom?

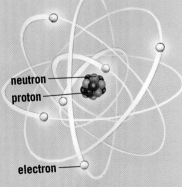

Atoms are made of three smaller particles: **protons, neutrons,** and **electrons.** Protons and neutrons stick together in the core, or **nucleus,** of an atom. Electrons fly around the nucleus in a constantly moving cloud. The identity of the atom depends on the number of protons in its nucleus. Hydrogen, for example, has one proton and one electron. Carbon, a bigger atom, has six protons and six electrons *(right).*

neutron

proton

electron

Eagle Nebula

Dense columns of **dust** and **gas** in the Eagle Nebula form a huge stellar nursery. The column at left is one **light-year** tall, one quarter of the distance between our Sun and the nearest star. Inside these clouds, stars are born when the thickest areas of hydrogen, helium, and carbon and silicon dust collapse into clumps and grow hotter and hotter. Some of these newborn stars can be seen between the dust columns.

What the Universe Is Made Of

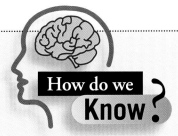

How do astronomers know what a star is made of when the star is so far away? How can they tell if it is moving toward or away from us? They study its light. A machine called a **spectrograph,** which is attached to a telescope *(below),* takes starlight and spreads it out into a **spectrum.** Each spectrum has its own pattern that astronomers analyse to learn about the star.

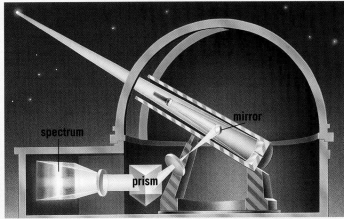

spectrum

mirror

prism

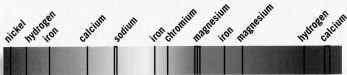

nickel hydrogen iron calcium sodium iron chromium magnesium iron magnesium hydrogen calcium

What Does Light Tell Us?

When a star's light passes through its **atmosphere,** gases in the atmosphere absorb some of the light. The resulting spectrum *(above)* will have dark lines that correspond to those gases. If the lines are pushed toward the red end of the spectrum, that tells us that the star is moving away. Lines pushed toward the blue end mean the star is racing toward us *(below).*

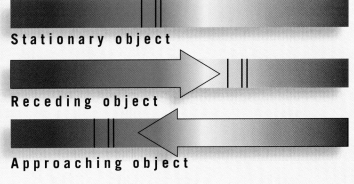

Stationary object

Receding object

Approaching object

What Is a Star?

H ot, bright, and far away, a **star** is a gigantic mass of glowing **gas**—mainly hydrogen and helium. The star's life span depends on how fast it turns its supply of hydrogen into helium.

So intense is the pressure deep inside a star that the **nuclei** of hydrogen **atoms** there start smashing into one another. This process, called **nuclear fusion,** throws off **energy** in the form of light and heat. It also produces helium.

Stars come in all colours and sizes. Some stars are thousands of times brighter than others. The Sun is an average star, but it stands out in one way: it has no companion (most stars occur in pairs, triples, or clusters). The Sun's closest stellar neighbour, Proxima Centauri, belongs to a triple-star group that shines bright just 4.3 **light-years** from Earth.

Starry Night

The four-starred Southern Cross *(right)* is visible mainly from the Southern Hemisphere. At its base is Acrux, the 14th-brightest star in the night sky. Because of their differing sizes and distances from Earth, stars vary from faint white pinpricks of light to blazing blue or yellow globes.

People   Stars on Earth

A stellar group of researchers gather for a portrait at the Harvard College Observatory in 1925. Antonia Maury *(third from left)* created a system of sorting stars based on the **spectrum,** or characteristic **wavelengths** of light, that each one emits.

Annie Jump Cannon *(fifth from left)* improved this system in 1898; by then, she had studied the spectra of 1,122 stars. Cannon's system, still used today, helped other astronomers make many important discoveries about stars and galaxies.

Bright? Or Just Nearby?

How bright a star looks depends on how bright the star really is, how far it is from Earth, and how much dust lies between the star and Earth. Two stars that seem equally bright *(below, left)* may in fact be a bright, distant star next to a dim, close star. The two stars have the same **apparent brightness,** but one has a greater **absolute brightness.** If two stars are equally far away *(right),* the star with the greater absolute brightness will have the greater apparent brightness too.

Size Matters

Stars vary in size from tiny neutron stars just 30 km (19 miles) across to red super- giants nearly 1 billion km (602 million miles) in diameter. For example, Sirius B, a white dwarf, has a diameter of 53,000 km (32,000 miles)— hardly larger than Uranus. The super-giant Betelgeuse, by contrast, is so huge that astronomers can make out features on its surface *(page 26)*—despite the fact that it is 500 light-years away.

Supergiant

Red Giant

Blue Main Sequence Star

Yellow Dwarf

Red Dwarf

White Dwarf

Hertzsprung-Russell Diagram

The Hertzsprung-Russell diagram *(below)* shows the link between a star's temperature and its luminosity—the amount of light the star actually gives off. More than 90 percent of stars—the Sun included—fall within a narrow band known as the main sequence. Other stars, including dim white dwarfs and bright red giants and supergiants, fall outside the main sequence —a clue to the fact that they are at later stages in their lives.

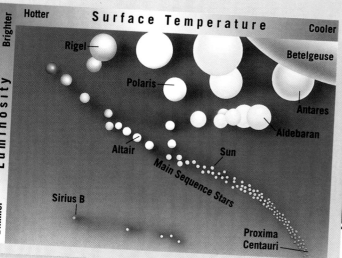

Brighter / Dimmer

Hotter / Cooler

Surface Temperature

Luminosity

Rigel

Polaris

Betelgeuse

Antares

Aldebaran

Altair

Sun

Main Sequence Stars

Sirius B

Proxima Centauri

Life Cycle of a Star

A Giant's Violent Death

Stars are not alive, but they pass through stages defined as birth, life, and death. Like you, a **star** changes radically during its life. Unlike you, a star is in existence for millions or billions of years. Most of the red giants and white dwarfs in the night sky, for example, were born before the Sun existed.

Stars are born in **nebulae**—that is, giant clouds of interstellar **dust** and **gas,** mostly hydrogen. **Gravity** pulls together vast amounts of this gas, forming a dense, spinning cloud. The hydrogen **atoms** then start colliding with one another, which heats them up. Eventually the centre of the cloud reaches 15,000,000°C (27,000,000°F) and forms the **core** of a **star.** The newborn star ignites and starts to burn, or shine. How long it will continue to do so depends on how much **mass** the star contained at its birth. The more massive the star, the shorter its life.

After shining for millions of years, a large star—one at least six times more massive than the Sun—begins to burn out. As its core runs out of hydrogen, the star expands into a red supergiant. The supergiant then contracts for the next few million years until suddenly exploding in a brilliant flash called a **supernova.** If the remaining core is small, it collapses into a dense neutron star. If the remaining core is large, however, it collapses even further to form a black hole.

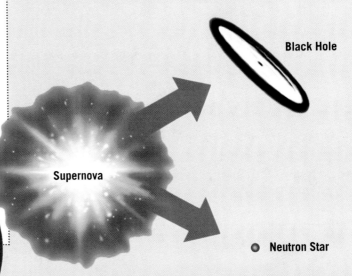

Black Hole

Supernova

Neutron Star

Red Supergiant

Red Giant

Blue Main Sequence Star

Life of an Average Star

An average star—one equal to or smaller than the Sun—lives longer and dies a less violent death than a large star. The Sun, for example, will burn for another five billion years before its core runs out of hydrogen. Its outer layers will then expand and cool, forming a red giant. In the end, the outer layers will drift away and the core will collapse into a dense white dwarf. Though a white dwarf is hot enough to glow, it eventually cools into a dead star called a black dwarf.

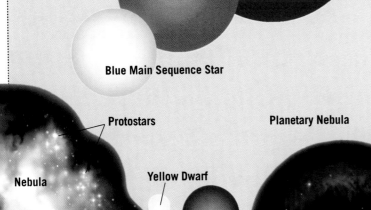

Protostars

Planetary Nebula

Nebula

Yellow Dwarf

Red Giant

White Dwarf   **Black Dwarf**

A Star Is Born

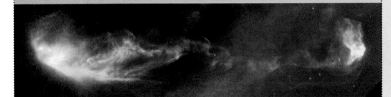

A hot jet of gas 5 trillion km (3 trillion miles) long shoots from a newborn star in this image captured by the Hubble Space Telescope. As the jet speeds through space it collides with interstellar gas, causing it to glow pink. The baby star, called a protostar, is hidden in the bright cloud seen at the left of the photograph.

Such interstellar clouds of gas and dust act as star nurseries that give birth to many, many stars. The birthing process creates a tremendous outflow of gas in the form of these jets. The reason for the jets is not fully understood, but scientists think they may be caused by energy that is released as the stars form.

People — Star of India

Subrahmanyan Chandrasekhar *(right)* set sail from India for England as a 20-year-old student in 1930. By the time his ship docked, Chandrasekhar had figured out that a star 1.44 times more massive than the Sun does not become a white dwarf as it dies. Instead, these stars continue to collapse. But he wasn't quite sure what they collapsed into. This work eventually led scientists to the discovery of black holes and neutron stars. For his work on the fate of stars larger than our Sun, Chandrasekhar won the Nobel Prize for Physics in 1983.

What's a Nebula?

The interstellar cloud of gas and dust known as a nebula can be the birthplace or the graveyard of a star. A nebula is so vast (some stretch tens of **light-years** across the universe) that it can often be seen through binoculars—or even with the naked eye. A gallery of these beautiful formations is shown below.

Emission

The Orion Nebula *(left)* is an emission nebula. Hot, young stars forming there produce so much **energy** that they make the gas of the nebula glow.

Reflection

The cloud around Rho Ophiuchi *(right, top)* and the cloud around Antares *(right, lower left)* are both known as reflection nebulae. Particles of dust inside each nebula reflect the light of nearby stars.

Dark

The Horsehead Nebula *(left)* is a dense cloud of gas and dust. It appears dark because it blocks out light from the emission nebula behind it.

Planetary

The Cat's Eye Nebula *(right)* is a sun-like star that died, shedding its outer layer of hydrogen gas. A planetary nebula is named for its circular shape; no planets are forming inside it.

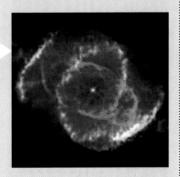

When Stars Get Old

The life span of a **star** depends on its appetite—for hydrogen, that is! A red dwarf—one of the smallest stars—can live for hundreds of billions of years because it consumes hydrogen **gas** at a slow rate. A medium star, by contrast, eats hydrogen much faster; its life expectancy is therefore 10 billion years or so. The largest star of all—a supergiant—runs through its fuel supply in just a few million years. The Sun, a medium star, is in no such danger: thanks to its average size (and average hunger for hydrogen), it will shine for another five billion years.

Once a medium star burns the last of its hydrogen, it may live for another 100 million years on the helium gas that formed in its **core** throughout its life. When this, too, is burned up, the medium star gradually shrinks into a white dwarf.

A massive star, by contrast, draws to a spectacular close: it explodes in a glorious supernova.

A Death in the Solar System

When the Sun begins to die (it is middle-aged now), its core will shrink while its outer layers expand. About five billion years from now, the Sun will balloon into a red giant, 100 times bigger and 500 times brighter than it is today. The Sun will swallow Mercury and Venus, then turn the Earth's surface into a soup of melted stone *(below)* 1,425°C (2,600°F) hot.

Your Local Supergiant

A hot spot pocks the face of Betelgeuse, a red supergiant, in a photo taken by the Hubble Space Telescope.

Betelgeuse *(left)*, a red supergiant, is probably the largest star in our corner of the Milky Way. The star is 500 **light-years** from Earth, but it is so large—1,000 times wider than the Sun—that it is the seventh-brightest star in the sky. If the Sun were as big as Betelgeuse, it would stretch to Jupiter.

Unlike the Sun with its small **sunspots,** Betelgeuse has one large, bright blotch on its surface. The spot is more than 10 times the size of Earth, but no one knows why it is there.

What's a Black Hole?

The death of a massive star—one whose remaining core is at least three times the mass of the Sun—produces a black hole, one of the most bizarre objects in the universe.

Absurdly small for its strength, a black hole exerts **gravity** so powerful that nothing —not even light—can escape from it.

'OK,' you're wondering, 'if no light escapes a black hole, how can we see one?' Well, we can't—at least not directly. Astronomers spot black holes by looking for the effect they have on objects nearby. When a black hole is near another star, for example, its gravity may pull gas from the star into a disk that spins around the black hole. The inner edge of the disk spins faster than the outer edge, creating friction and heat that send out x-rays detectable by **satellites** above Earth.

Heavy?

Neutron Star

Professor Dave Arnett holds a 1.3-cm (.5-in.) ball showing how small Sears Tower, in Chicago, USA, would become if you turned it into solid rock and compressed it to the **density** of a neutron star. The aftermath of a fiery **supernova,** a neutron star is only 30 km (19 miles) across.

Yet it is so dense that a single teaspoon of it would weigh 5 million tons.

Blue Supergiant

Black Hole

X-Rays

Discovering Neutron Stars

British astronomer Jocelyn Bell *(below)* stands amid the 1,000 antennas she set up near Cambridge in the late 1960s. She used these wooden poles strung with copper wire as a giant radio telescope. In 1967, Bell discovered an object deep in space that was emitting a radio wave every 1.33 seconds. A year later, other skygazers reported that Bell had found a neutron star—the first one ever detected. Spinning rapidly on its **axis,** a pulsing neutron star, or **pulsar,** sends out radio waves that sweep past Earth in a repeated beam of **energy.** From Earth, as in the sequence below, the star seems to flash on and off.

What Is a Supernova?

The final moments in the life of a massive **star** are a complete catastrophe. In less than one-tenth of a second, all that's left of the star—a gaseous iron **core** much smaller than Earth—collapses at high speed, creating a compact ball just 100 km (62 miles) across. In that instant, the star releases 100 times more **energy** than the Sun has radiated in its entire lifetime. Most of that energy takes the form of neutrinos—chargeless particles with little mass that race through space at near the speed of light.

The core then contracts still further, forming a ball no more than 20 km (12 miles) in diameter. By now, the temperature at its core has reached 170,000,000°C (306,000,000°F). The in-falling layers crash onto the collapsed core at one-fourth the speed of light, causing the star to explode in a brilliant flash called a **supernova.**

1984

1987

All was quiet in the Tarantula Nebula—a cloud of **gas** and **dust** in a **galaxy** near Earth—when astronomers photographed it in 1984 *(above)*. Then, on February 24, 1987, skygazers noticed that a star known as a blue supergiant had gone supernova—that is, exploded—at the nebula's edge *(right)*. Unlike the fast-fading supernovas that scientists had studied before, this one—dubbed Supernova 1987A—took 85 days to reach maximum brightness. Three years later *(bottom right)*, Supernova 1987A was still visible to the Hubble Space Telescope. By then, energy from the explosion had lit up material *(green ring)* surrounding the old star.

Then & NOW!

Bright Light, Ancient Sky

A star so bright that it could be seen during the day appeared in the sky for 23 days in the year 1054. Among those who observed the mysterious light were Native Americans living in what is now New Mexico, USA; they captured the sight as a pictograph, or rock painting *(top)*. Modern astronomers believe that the light was caused by a supernova, traces of which are still visible today as the Crab Nebula *(above)*.

A Deep-Space Detonation

1990

Supernova 1987A was detected by both man and machine. Ian Shelton, an astronomer working at an observatory in Chile, spotted the supernova in a photo he took of the Large Magellanic Cloud (a nearby galaxy) on February 24, 1987. Thinking the unexpected star was an error, Shelton raced outside. There in the night sky, below the Tarantula Nebula, was the supernova—the brightest seen in 383 years. Shelton's colleague, Oscar Duhalde, had also noticed the new star two hours earlier. The very first evidence, however, had come even earlier: an underwater neutrino detector in Ohio, USA, had collected particles from the supernova the day before it became visible (no one checked the machine until after Shelton's report).

Ian Shelton *(above)* shot one of the first photos of Supernova 1987A at Las Campanas Observatory in Chile. Oscar Duhalde *(below)* co-discovered the supernova.

A diver inspects some of the 2,048 light sensors lining the walls of a neutrino detector 600 m (2,000 ft.) beneath Lake Erie, on the US-Canada border. This device detected eight neutrinos from Supernova 1987A.

What Is a Galaxy?

A **galaxy** is a huge collection of **dust, gas,** and **stars.** Formed soon after the birth of the universe and held together by **gravity** since then, a galaxy is constantly voyaging through space.

Galaxies vary in size. The smallest may contain a few million stars, while the biggest may have a trillion. As shown at right, they also come in a wide range of shapes. Some galaxies look like irregular globs of stars; others resemble footballs, rugby balls, or tight spirals.

One such spiral galaxy is our own—the Milky Way. The Sun nestles in one of its spiral arms. The Milky Way's nearest galactic neighbour—the Sagittarius dwarf galaxy, about 60,000 **light-years** from Earth—cannot be seen with the naked eye. That's because it lies behind the central bulge of the Milky Way—and is slowly being swallowed by it!

What's in a Name?

The Sombrero Galaxy *(below)* is one of many galaxies nicknamed for their looks. Others include the Whirlpool, the Spindle, and the Antennae. Edwin Hubble was the first astronomer to classify galaxies based on their appearance *(see gallery at right)*. Today, a newly discovered galaxy is often named by—or for—the person who found it. Others, such as NGC 1365, are known only by letters and numbers.

A Gallery of Galaxies

Spiral

Spiral galaxies, such as M83 *(right)* and the Milky Way, have a large, flat disk and spiral arms containing bright young stars. A central bulge is home to older stars.

Barred Spiral

A bright band, or bar, of stars runs through the middle of some spiral galaxies, including NGC 1365 *(left)*. The spiral arms appear to extend from the ends of the bars, not from the centre.

Elliptical

Disk-shaped elliptical galaxies, like M87 *(right)*, are the most common regular galaxies. They are also very old; most of their light comes from stars that are red giants.

Irregular

Some galaxies, such as the Large Magellanic Cloud *(left)*, are called irregular because they have no clear shape. An irregular galaxy is often sprinkled with young blue stars and clouds of dust and gas.

The Milky Way

All stars are local—that is, every star you can see in the night sky belongs to our galaxy, the Milky Way. A great spiral that is 100,000 light-years across, the Milky Way has about 200 billion stars—including the Sun. Our solar system lies about 30,000 light-years from the galaxy's centre, in a spiral limb known as the Orion Arm. When the Milky Way is viewed from the side, its bulging centre *(below)* becomes clearly visible.

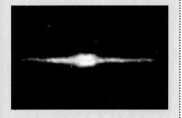

Strange But TRUE !

Dark Matter

On a clear, dark night, the sky seems filled with stars *(above)*. What you can't see, however, makes up 90 percent of the **mass** in the universe. Dark matter, as this mysterious substance is known, shows itself only through the gravity it exerts on galaxies.

What is dark matter? Could it be millions of black holes? Probably not. Billions of **planets** the size of Jupiter? Perhaps. A new type of subatomic particle zipping through the universe? Quite possibly. So far, no one really knows.

When Galaxies Collide

A head-on crash between two galaxies would be an interstellar smash-up of colossal proportions. The Hubble Space Telescope captured just such a collision in 1997, when it took pictures showing the run-in of two galaxies known as the Antennae *(below)*. The accident was not purely destructive: as the galaxies ram each other, clouds of gas and dust inside them merge to trigger the birth of new stars.

What's a Quasar?

Quasars are the most energetic objects in the universe. Shining with the energy of 1,000 galaxies, a **quasar** may be the active centre of a young but incredibly distant galaxy, fuelled by massive amounts of matter disappearing into a gigantic black hole. Shown below is 3C273, the brightest quasar seen from Earth; it is 1.8 billion light-years away.

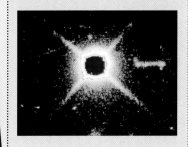

Stargazing

As if they were doing a connect-the-dots puzzle in the sky, early stargazers imagined that the **stars** outlined pictures of animals, people, and ideas. These fanciful groupings of stars are called **constellations.** The ancient Greeks named 48 constellations; over time, other skywatchers added 40 more.

If you want to see what they saw, you're in luck: the majority of constellations are visible at most times of the year. Because of the Earth's rotation, however, different constellations come into view at different hours of the night. The later you stay up, the more you'll see.

For the ancients, observing the heavens was much more than just a hobby. Seafarers used star charts to cross oceans. Spiritual leaders believed the positions of the stars could help explain the mysteries of life—and foretell the future. The stars continue to entice us today.

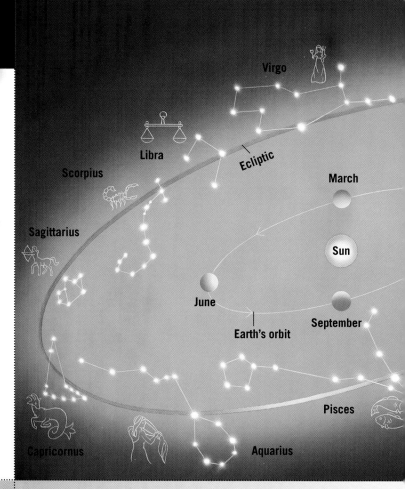

Virgo
Libra
Scorpius
Ecliptic
March
Sagittarius
Sun
June
September
Earth's orbit
Pisces
Capricornus
Aquarius

What's Astrology?

Astrology, from the Greek words for 'star' and 'science', was developed by many ancient cultures as a way of explaining events by the positions of the stars and **planets.** Even today, astrologers believe that a person's personality and future are determined by the position of the planets, the Sun, and the Moon at the instant of his or her birth. Astronomers, however, do not take astrology seriously; they consider it a superstition, *not* a 'star science'.

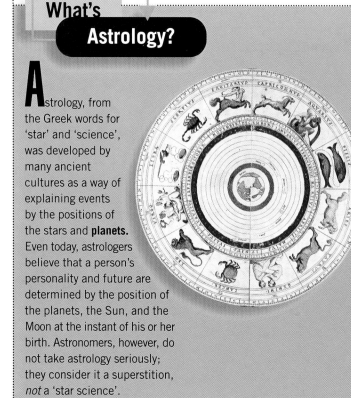

Seeing Stars in Other Lands

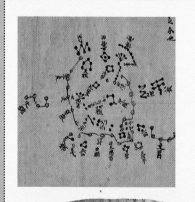

The Big Dipper stands out at the bottom of the ancient Chinese star map shown at left. The Chinese—like almost every early human culture—believed the stars held clues to the mysteries of life. They drew up star maps with 28 sectors, each containing its own constellations.

Many Native Americans, too, named constellations of their own. Some recorded these formations on ceremonial star charts made of deer-skin *(left).*

The Zodiac

Twelve constellations, spread evenly through the sky, form the zodiac *(left)*. ('Zodiac' comes from the Greek word for 'circle of animals'.) The Earth's **orbit** around the Sun matches an imaginary line, called the ecliptic, that connects all 12 constellations of the zodiac. As the Earth moves around the Sun over the course of a year, different constellations become visible from the planet. To an observer on Earth, this makes it seem that the constellations of the zodiac are marching across the night sky. A different zodiacal constellation appears roughly overhead each month.

Polaris: The Pole Star

Learn this simple trick—how to find north without a compass—and you will be able to find constellations in the night sky. First, find the seven stars of the Big Dipper *(above, right)*, which looks like a saucepan with a bent handle. Imagine a line running through the two outermost stars of the pan; this line should head from the pan bottom to its top. Follow this line until it meets Polaris, the North Star. Now face Polaris; north will be in front of you, south behind you, east to your right, and west to your left. At the North Pole, Polaris seems fixed overhead, and the other stars appear to spin around it *(time-lapse photo, above)*.

'Round the Pole They Go!

Stars and constellations that appear in the northern sky throughout the year, circling Polaris once every 24 hours, are known as circumpolar stars. They include the Big Dipper (also called Ursa Major, the Great Bear); the Little Dipper (Ursa Minor, the Little Bear); Cassiopeia, the Queen; Draco, the Dragon; and Cepheus, the King. Circumpolar stars appear in different parts of the northern sky depending on the time of year.

What's a Constellation?

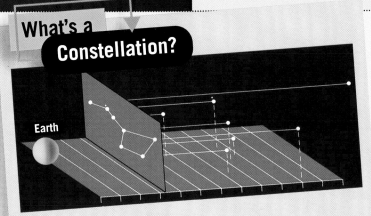

A constellation is a group of stars, such as the Big Dipper *(above)*, that look close together. In fact, they may be very far apart. This optical illusion occurs because humans cannot see distant objects in three dimensions. Thus the star at the tip of the Big Dipper's handle looks close to the star next to it, but the first is 198 **light-years** from Earth and the second is only 78 light-years from Earth. Seen from the side, as shown above, the stars would be nowhere near one another. What do you think the Big Dipper would look like in another galaxy?

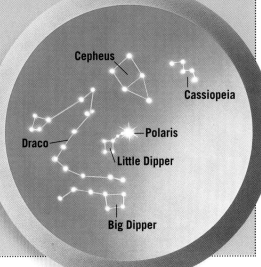

Winter Constellations

Winter, with its clear, calm air and its trees free of leaves, is an ideal time to stargaze. Once you have learned to recognize the **constellation** Orion, the Hunter, use it as a guide to pinpoint other major winter constellations. These include Orion's hunting hounds: Canis Major, the Big Dog, and Canis Minor, the Little Dog. Sirius, the brightest star in the sky, is also called the Dog Star because it is in Canis Major.

In Greek legend, Orion's pursuit of the seven sisters known as the Pleiades led Artemis (goddess of the hunt) to kill Orion and place him in the sky as a constellation. In reality, the Pleiades are a star cluster near Taurus, the Bull. Six or seven **stars** in the Pleiades are visible to the naked eye; astronomers believe the cluster contains up to 500 young stars, all less than 100 million years old.

A Hunter, a Dog, and a Bull

Becoming an expert stargazer takes patience and practice, but the star chart below will help you get started. With Polaris above and behind you at 9:00 p.m. in winter, face south and find Orion (look for the three stars in his belt). Then, using Orion's belt as an arrow pointing down and to the left, pick out Sirius, the brightest star in the night sky. Sirius is also called the Dog Star because it anchors the constellation Canis Major, the Big Dog. Orion's belt—pointing up and to the right, this time—will also guide you to Aldebaran, the brightest star in the constellation Taurus, the Bull.

Orion, the Hunter

It is fairly easy to find the constellation Orion *(right)*. Three stars in a row make up Orion's belt; 'hanging' from his belt are three fainter stars that form his sword. Both Orion's

right shoulder (the red star Betelgeuse) and his left ankle (the blue white star Rigel) shine bright in the winter sky.

Ancient Greek astronomers showed Orion as a hunter *(left)*, or as an archer drawing his bow. Other cultures took a different view. The Egyptians saw this group of stars as the outline of their god Osiris; the Pawnee Indians of North America saw the three lined-up stars as a trio of running deer.

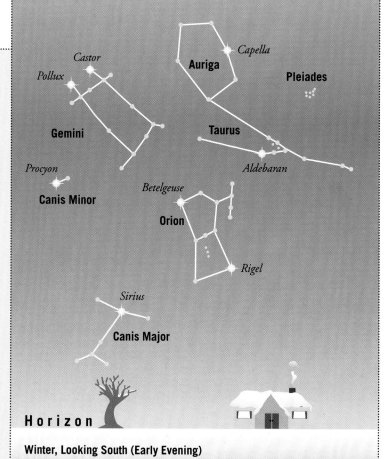

Castor
Pollux
Gemini
Procyon
Canis Minor
Capella
Auriga
Pleiades
Taurus
Aldebaran
Betelgeuse
Orion
Rigel
Sirius
Canis Major

Horizon

Winter, Looking South (Early Evening)

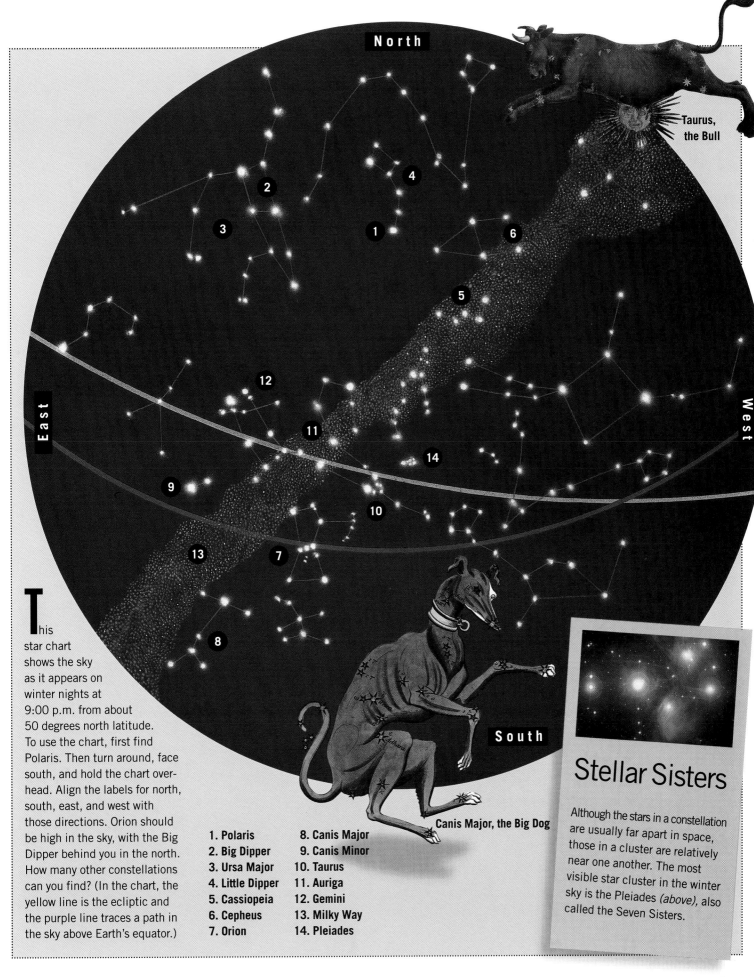

North

Taurus, the Bull

2

4

3

1

6

5

12

11

14

9

10

East

West

13

7

8

Canis Major, the Big Dog

South

This star chart shows the sky as it appears on winter nights at 9:00 p.m. from about 50 degrees north latitude. To use the chart, first find Polaris. Then turn around, face south, and hold the chart overhead. Align the labels for north, south, east, and west with those directions. Orion should be high in the sky, with the Big Dipper behind you in the north. How many other constellations can you find? (In the chart, the yellow line is the ecliptic and the purple line traces a path in the sky above Earth's equator.)

1. Polaris
2. Big Dipper
3. Ursa Major
4. Little Dipper
5. Cassiopeia
6. Cepheus
7. Orion
8. Canis Major
9. Canis Minor
10. Taurus
11. Auriga
12. Gemini
13. Milky Way
14. Pleiades

Stellar Sisters

Although the stars in a constellation are usually far apart in space, those in a cluster are relatively near one another. The most visible star cluster in the winter sky is the Pleiades *(above)*, also called the Seven Sisters.

Spring Constellations

The spring sky is spangled with the victims of Hercules. In early March, as the winter **constellations** vanish in the west, three constellations named for foes of Hercules show up in the east.

The easiest of these to spot is Leo the Lion, which appears just below the Big Dipper. Leo's tough hide supposedly made the lion invincible, but Hercules strangled the beast—and wore its pelt as a trophy ever after.

Hercules also killed the many-headed Hydra. In legend, this serpent grew two new heads to replace any that were cut off. In **astronomy,** Hydra, the Water Snake, is the longest constellation visible in spring.

A third new arrival in the spring sky is Cancer, the Crab; a sidekick of the Hydra, it too was slain by Hercules. Cancer the constellation is hard to find—it has no bright **stars**—but the hunt is well worth it: using a small telescope, you may be able to make out Cancer's spectacular star cluster, the Beehive. Many stars in the Beehive are doubles or triples.

Leo, the Lion

Leo the Lion is easy to spot: the bright stars that form its head and chest also make a backward question mark in the sky. (Regulus, the constellation's brightest star, marks Leo's front foot.) Another way to find Leo is to look for the triangle of stars that trace the lion's hindquarters; the star Denebola forms the tip of Leo's tail.

In legend, Leo was a fierce lion whose skin was so thick no weapon could pierce it. Hercules got around this by strangling the beast. But even in death, Leo was so majestic that the gods put him in the heavens.

The Lion and the Herdsman

To spot constellations in the spring sky, first find the Big Dipper; it should be almost directly overhead. Trace a path downward from the Dipper's bowl until you come to Leo, sitting high in the sky. Next, follow Leo's tail to the left (the southeast) to spot Spica, the brightest star in Virgo.

The brightest star in the spring sky, however, is not in Virgo. To find it, use your imagination to extend the curve of the Big Dipper's handle; this points the way to a brilliant golden orange star, Arcturus—then you can find Boötes, the Herdsman.

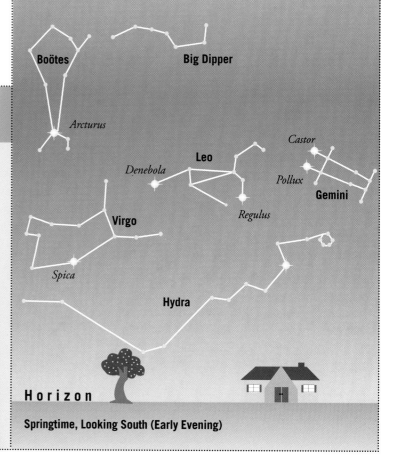

Boötes — Big Dipper — Arcturus — Castor — Leo — Denebola — Pollux — Gemini — Regulus — Virgo — Spica — Hydra — **Horizon**

Springtime, Looking South (Early Evening)

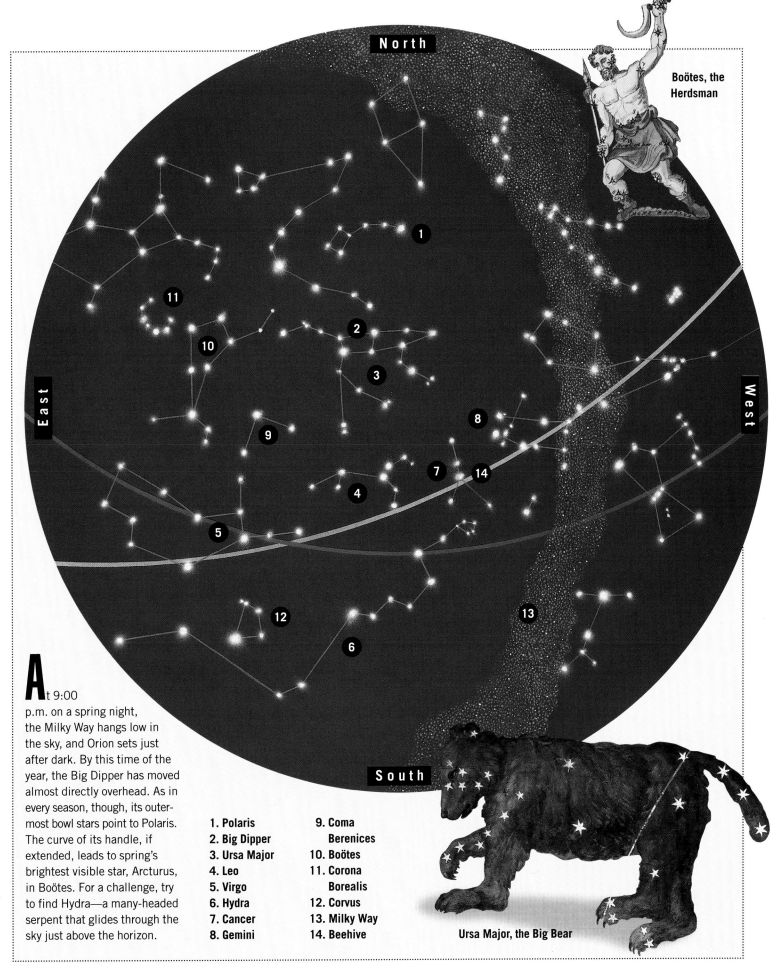

Boötes, the Herdsman

North

East

West

South

At 9:00 p.m. on a spring night, the Milky Way hangs low in the sky, and Orion sets just after dark. By this time of the year, the Big Dipper has moved almost directly overhead. As in every season, though, its outermost bowl stars point to Polaris. The curve of its handle, if extended, leads to spring's brightest visible star, Arcturus, in Boötes. For a challenge, try to find Hydra—a many-headed serpent that glides through the sky just above the horizon.

1. Polaris
2. Big Dipper
3. Ursa Major
4. Leo
5. Virgo
6. Hydra
7. Cancer
8. Gemini
9. Coma Berenices
10. Boötes
11. Corona Borealis
12. Corvus
13. Milky Way
14. Beehive

Ursa Major, the Big Bear

Summer Constellations

A never-ending chase takes place in the summer sky. As spring comes to a close, Orion, the Hunter, sets in the west—pursued, legend has it, by Scorpius, the Scorpion, rising in the east. In myth, Orion boasted of being able to kill every animal on Earth. This alarmed Gaia, the goddess of Earth, who sent a giant scorpion after Orion. In a brief but fierce battle, the arachnid killed the hunter with a sting to the heel. The gods then gave both combatants honoured places in the heavens—but they put them on opposite sides of the sky to keep them from fighting again.

The most brilliant **star** in the summer sky is Vega, in the **constellation** Lyra. Harder to find is Hercules, a dim and sprawling constellation. It contains M13—a bright globular cluster that is home to at least one million stars.

Hercules, a Crown, and a Scorpion

Summertime . . . and the viewing's not easy! That's because summer constellations have fewer bright stars than those visible in the spring. The warmer weather, though, lets you scan the sky at leisure. Start by facing south and finding the three bright stars—Altair, Deneb, and Vega—that make up the Summer Triangle. From Vega, trace a line almost due west to find the brilliant golden orange star Arcturus, in the constellation Boötes. Now backtrack a bit to the east until you spot Corona Borealis, a semi-circle of seven stars. Hercules can be dim, so look first for the Keystone—four bright stars that form his torso. Scorpius lurks far below the feet of Hercules, near the horizon.

Scorpius, the Scorpion

Called 'brilliant', 'splendid', even 'exquisite' by astronomers, Scorpius, the Scorpion, crawls along the southern horizon on summer evenings—the hours from about dusk to midnight. If you live above 47 degrees north latitude, part of the scorpion's tail will be hidden from view; if you live above 52 degrees north latitude, you will not be able to see it at all. In addition to its unmistakable shape *(left)*, Scorpius is noted for its reddish orange heart, the red supergiant star Antares. With a diameter of 1,000 million km (600 million miles), Antares is about 700 times wider than the Sun.

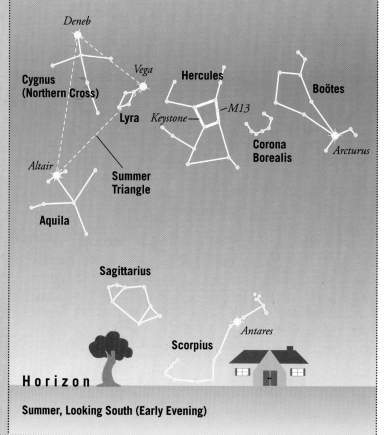

Summer, Looking South (Early Evening)

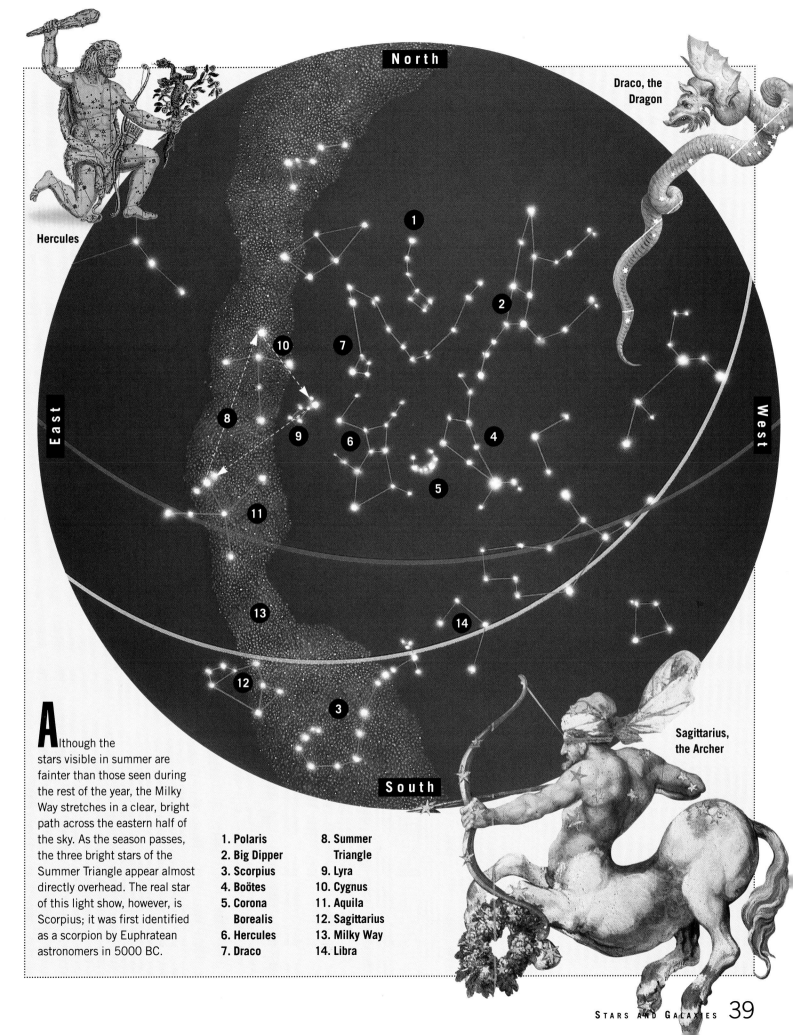

North

Draco, the
Dragon

Hercules

East

West

Sagittarius,
the Archer

South

Although the
stars visible in summer are
fainter than those seen during
the rest of the year, the Milky
Way stretches in a clear, bright
path across the eastern half of
the sky. As the season passes,
the three bright stars of the
Summer Triangle appear almost
directly overhead. The real star
of this light show, however, is
Scorpius; it was first identified
as a scorpion by Euphratean
astronomers in 5000 BC.

1. Polaris
2. Big Dipper
3. Scorpius
4. Boötes
5. Corona
   Borealis
6. Hercules
7. Draco
8. Summer
   Triangle
9. Lyra
10. Cygnus
11. Aquila
12. Sagittarius
13. Milky Way
14. Libra

Autumn Constellations

Pegasus, the Winged Horse, takes centre stage in autumn. Pegasus can be difficult to spot because the creature flies inverted. To find it, look for four bright **stars** that seem to form a square; these make up the 'Great Square'. Near Pegasus is the **constellation** Andromeda, a girl rescued by Pegasus in Greek myth. Andromeda contains M31, the closest spiral galaxy to Earth—and a near twin of our own Milky Way.

Autumn skygazing can make you feel waterlogged: there is Pisces, the Fish; Capricornus, the Sea Goat; and Cetus, the Whale. In the tail of that whale is Mira, a variable star; Mira seems to fade, disappear, then reappear as the year goes by. The Summer Triangle, with its bright stars Vega, Deneb, and Altair, is still visible in the western sky.

Horses That Fly and Goats That Swim

In autumn, a bright reddish star called Fomalhaut shows up near the southern horizon (though viewers in the UK and at other latitudes above 50 degrees north will not quite be able to see it). Above Fomalhaut lies Pegasus, the Winged Horse; west of Fomalhaut is Capricornus, the Sea Goat.

Stargazing in the autumn is especially exciting because it gives you a chance to see a **galaxy** 2.3 million **light-years** away—with the naked eye! Called M31 or the Andromeda galaxy, this spiral galaxy (a twin of our own) shows up as a fuzzy smudge or patch of light in the constellation Andromeda.

Pegasus, The Winged Horse

The Pegasus of myth *(below)* was a winged horse who carried lightning bolts for Zeus on Mount Olympus. The Pegasus of the autumn sky *(right)* can be hard to find because it 'flies' upside down. A bright white star named Markab—Arabic for 'saddle'—anchors the lower-right corner of the Great Square, or body, of Pegasus.

According to Greek legend, Pegasus was born from sea foam and the blood of Medusa, a snake-haired monster so ugly she turned onlookers to stone. Pegasus, though, was a force of good; he once created a magic fountain by striking the ground with his hoofs.

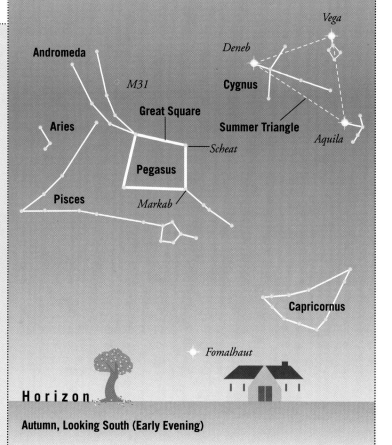

Autumn, Looking South (Early Evening)

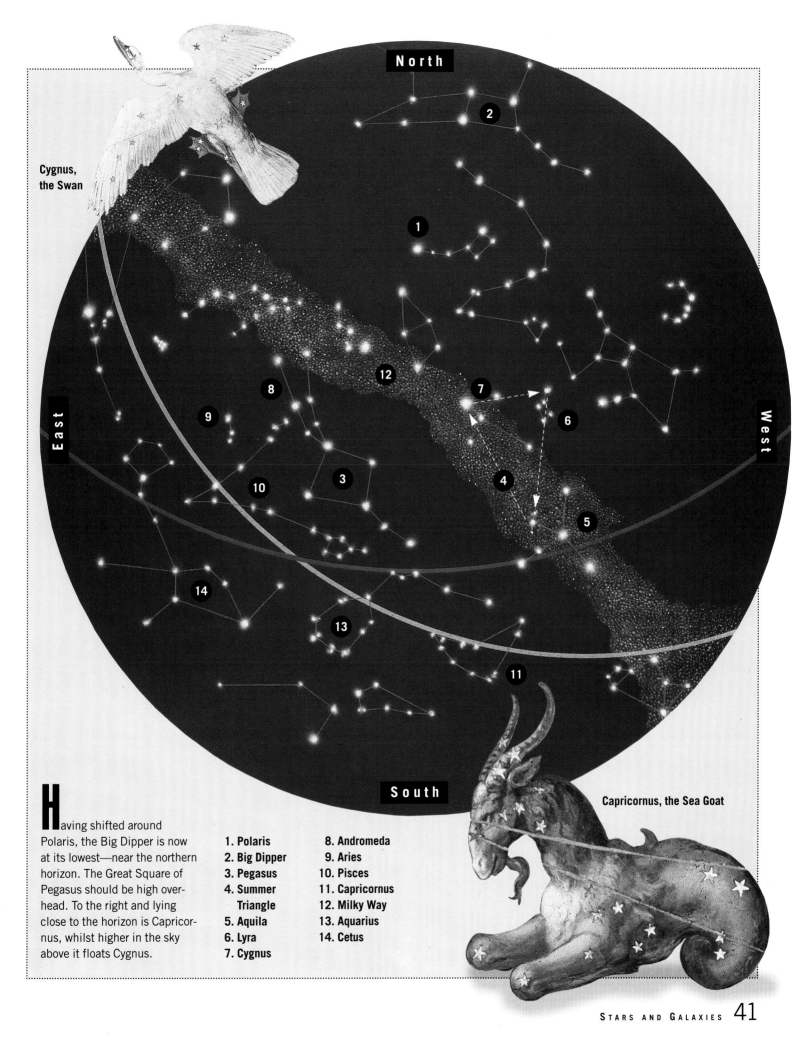

North

West

East

South

Cygnus,
the Swan

Capricornus, the Sea Goat

Having shifted around Polaris, the Big Dipper is now at its lowest—near the northern horizon. The Great Square of Pegasus should be high overhead. To the right and lying close to the horizon is Capricornus, whilst higher in the sky above it floats Cygnus.

1. Polaris
2. Big Dipper
3. Pegasus
4. Summer Triangle
5. Aquila
6. Lyra
7. Cygnus
8. Andromeda
9. Aries
10. Pisces
11. Capricornus
12. Milky Way
13. Aquarius
14. Cetus

What Is the Solar System?

The **solar system** is a collection of planets and other spinning, speeding objects revolving around a medium-sized star located in the Milky Way **galaxy.** It's a tiny speck of a place in the gigantic **universe.** If the universe were an endless ocean beach, the solar system would be just one grain of sand.

In the solar system, you'll find: 1 **star** (the Sun); 9 **planets;** 63 **moons** (at last count); 6 big asteroids at least 300 km (186 miles) in diameter; and vast numbers of smaller **asteroids, comets,** and **meteoroids.** Floating in the vast space between all of these objects are countless particles of **dust** and **gas,** known as interplanetary medium. The dust comes from comet tails and from colliding asteroids and meteoroids. The gas comes mostly from the **solar wind** that blows outward from the Sun.

The Sun is at the centre of the solar system. Its strong **gravity** tugs on the planets and keeps them from flying off into space. As the Sun travels through space it drags the planets and all the other objects in the solar system with it at a speed of about 20 km (10 miles) per second—many times faster than a speeding bullet!

What's in a Name?

Planet

The word 'planet' comes from 'planetai', an ancient Greek word that means 'wanderer'. In ancient times, people noticed that planets moved differently from the stars around them. Unlike stars, they did not seem to follow the same paths across the sky. Instead, they wandered through the heavens, appearing in different places at different times of the year. People thought it a bad omen when two or more planets appeared close together, as Venus *(top),* Jupiter *(below the moon),* and Mercury *(in the trees, low on the horizon)* do here.

Are there other solar systems?

Yes! Many stars are like the Sun and have their own planets. It is difficult for scientists to see these planets directly, even through the strongest telescope. The planets are hidden by the glare of the bright stars they orbit. But scientists can see the stars. By studying how a star appears to 'wobble' they can sometimes tell if it has a planet. One star thought to have a planet forming is Beta Pictoris *(right),* located about 50 light-years from the Sun.

How **Big?**

Solar System

Scientists measure distances in the solar system in **astronomical units (AUs).** One AU is the distance between Earth and the Sun—about 150 million km (93 million miles). It is 40 AU from the Sun to Pluto. But the solar system does not stop there. Some 50,000 to 100,000 AUs from the Sun is an icy zone known as the **Oort cloud.** This is the true boundary of our solar system and where scientists believe many comets come from.

Sun

Oort Cloud

The Nine Planets

Our solar system has nine planets. The planet closest to the Sun is Mercury. Then come Venus, Earth, Mars, Jupiter, Saturn, Uranus, Neptune, and Pluto. The planets form a huge disk around the Sun because they **orbit,** or circle, the Sun on nearly the same flat plane as Earth. Most of the orbits are almost exact circles. Pluto, however, has a very **elliptical** orbit. During part of its orbit (which takes 248 Earth years), Pluto swings closer to the Sun than its neighbour Neptune.

How Did the Solar System Form?

The **solar system** began as a cloud of cosmic **dust** and **gas** drifting in the outer reaches of the Milky Way **galaxy.** About 4.6 billion years ago, many scientists believe the cloud was slammed into by a gigantic shock wave from an exploding **star.** This caused the cloud to collapse into a flat, spinning disk. As the cloud collapsed, its dust and gases spiralled toward its centre to form a dense and incredibly hot

core. Finally, the core got so hot that it set off a continuous nuclear reaction—our Sun was born. Meanwhile, the leftover gas and dust in the spinning cloud clumped together to form the nine **planets.** What did not form into planets became **asteroids** and **comets** instead.

The cloud's core finally got hot enough to ignite. A star—our Sun—was born. A fierce **solar wind** blew away much of the dust and gases around the newborn rocky planets. A dusty ring circling the infant Earth *(below)* would over time be swept up by the planet.

4

3

Tiny dust particles in the cloud began to stick together, some growing into clumps up to several kilometres across. The biggest clumps became planetesimals— the building blocks of planets. Attracted by **gravity,** they collided with one another to create still larger bodies. Over millions of years, these bodies grew into the nine planets. Far from the Sun, frigid temperatures allowed gases to collect around some, eventually forming the four gas giants.

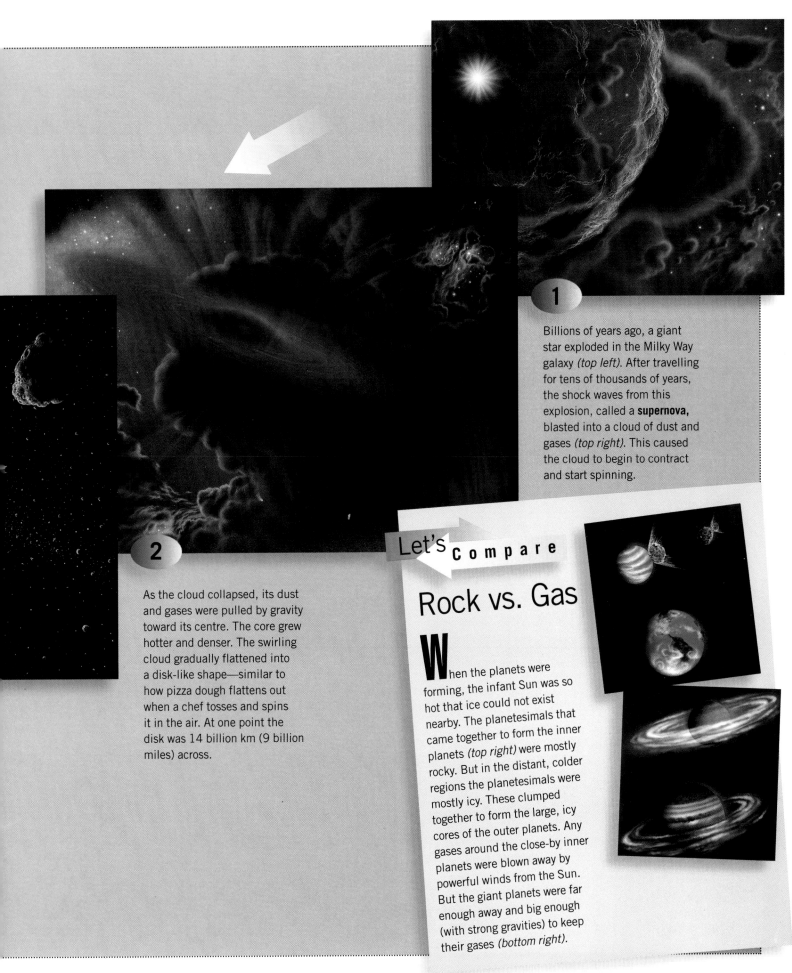

1

Billions of years ago, a giant star exploded in the Milky Way galaxy *(top left)*. After travelling for tens of thousands of years, the shock waves from this explosion, called a **supernova,** blasted into a cloud of dust and gases *(top right)*. This caused the cloud to begin to contract and start spinning.

2

As the cloud collapsed, its dust and gases were pulled by gravity toward its centre. The core grew hotter and denser. The swirling cloud gradually flattened into a disk-like shape—similar to how pizza dough flattens out when a chef tosses and spins it in the air. At one point the disk was 14 billion km (9 billion miles) across.

Let's **Compare**

Rock vs. Gas

When the planets were forming, the infant Sun was so hot that ice could not exist nearby. The planetesimals that came together to form the inner planets *(top right)* were mostly rocky. But in the distant, colder regions the planetesimals were mostly icy. These clumped together to form the large, icy cores of the outer planets. Any gases around the close-by inner planets were blown away by powerful winds from the Sun. But the giant planets were far enough away and big enough (with strong gravities) to keep their gases *(bottom right)*.

Solar System Close up

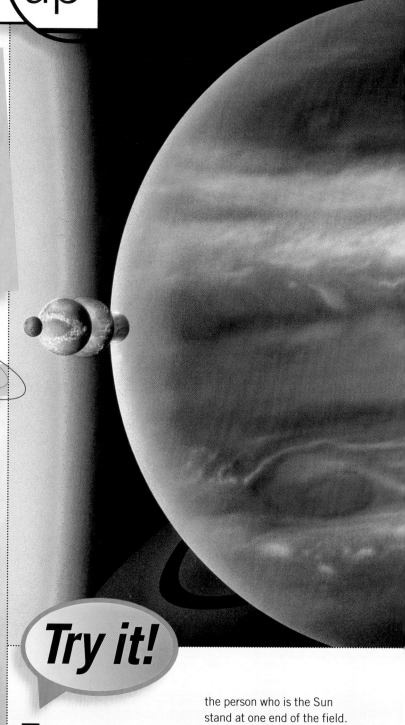

Let's Compare

Planet Sizes

Size-wise, the **planets** in the **solar system** can be divided into two main groups: regular and humongous. The 'regulars' include the four rocky inner planets—Mercury, Venus, Earth, and Mars—and Pluto. The 'humongous' are the four gas giants: Jupiter, Saturn, Uranus, and Neptune. Jupiter is the biggest. In fact, 1,400 Earths could easily fit inside Jupiter. All the planets are teeny compared with the Sun. Here's one way to think about it: if the Sun were a football, Earth would be a pinhead and Jupiter would be about the size of a 10 pence piece.

Fast FACTS

Largest Planet Jupiter, with a diameter of 139,822 km (86,885 miles)

Smallest Planet Pluto, with a diameter of about 2,274 km (1,413 miles)

Densest Planet Earth, with an average density about 5.5 times that of water

Lightest Planet Saturn, with an average density of about 0.68 times that of water; $\frac{1}{8}$ that of Earth

Fastest Planet Mercury, which orbits the Sun at an average speed of 172,408 km/h (107,132 mph)

Planet with Most Moons Saturn (18, and maybe more)

Planet with Longest Day Venus, with 243 Earth days

Planet with Shortest Day Jupiter, with about 10 Earth hours

Planet with Tallest Volcano Mars, with Olympus Mons, which is 29 km (18 miles) high

Hottest Planet Venus, with an estimated average surface temperature of 500°C (900°F)

Coldest Planet Pluto, with an estimated average surface temperature of between -228°C and -238°C (-378°F and -396°F)

Largest Asteroid Ceres, 913 km (567 miles) across

Closest Star Proxima Centauri, about 4.3 light-years from Earth

Try it!

To experience the distances between planets, try this activity. You'll need 10 people, a measuring tape, and an open field that's at least 30 m (100 ft.) long. Everyone should choose to 'be' either the Sun or one of the nine planets. Have the person who is the Sun stand at one end of the field. Let 31 cm (1 ft.) equal about 58 million km (36 million miles). Space your planets according to the measurements in the chart at right. The planets should be in the following order, starting from the Sun: Mercury, Venus, Earth, Mars, Jupiter, Saturn, Uranus, Neptune, and Pluto.

Sun
0 m
(0 ft.)

Mercury
31cm
(1 ft.)

Venus
62 cm
(2 ft.)

Earth
92 cm
(3 ft.)

Mars
1 m
(4 ft.)

Jupiter
4 m
(13 ft.)

Saturn
8 m
(25 ft.)

Uranus
15 m
(50 ft.)

Neptune
24 m
(78 ft.)

Pluto
31 m
(102 ft.)

1 in. = 2.564 cm
1 ft. = .3048 m

The Sun Our Star

O ur Sun is really a very ordinary **star.** Compared with other stars, it's not particularly large. Nor is it particularly hot. Yet, from our perspective on Earth, the Sun is just the right size and temperature. If it were much bigger, it would have exploded long ago. If it were much smaller, it would not produce enough heat and light to sustain life on Earth.

That heat and light—or **energy**—is created in the Sun's **core** by a natural process called **nuclear fusion,** which creates an enormous release of tiny bits of light energy, called **photons.** It takes photons up to 10 million years to reach the Sun's surface, but only eight minutes to travel from there to Earth. Just think about it. The sunlight you see right now was actually created 10 million years ago!

Caution: Never Look Directly at the Sun

Fast FACTS

- **Temperature** 6,000°C (11,000°F) at surface; 15,000,000°C (27,000,000°F) at core

- **Distance Across** 1,392,000 km (864,900 miles), or 109 times Earth's diameter

- **Mass** 2 million trillion trillion kg (4.4 million trillion trillion lb.), or 330,000 times Earth's mass; the Sun makes up 99.9 percent of the mass of the entire solar system

- **Gravity** 28 times as great as gravity on Earth; a 45-kg (100-lb.) Earthling would weigh 1,270 kg (2,800 lb.) on the Sun

- **Luminosity** 390 billion billion megawatts, energy equal to 90 billion 1-megaton hydrogen bombs going off every second; the Sun is 600,000 times brighter than the full Moon

- **Density** 0.256 that of Earth

- **Time for One Rotation** 27 days at equator; 34 days at poles

Corona

The **corona,** a wispy halo of superhot gases, is the outermost layer of the Sun's atmosphere. It stretches for more than 1 million km (620,000 miles) into space and is always expanding and changing its shape.

Chromosphere

This layer of the Sun's atmosphere is where all the solar fireworks take place. Fiery jets of gas called spicules leap to heights of 9,000 km (6,000 miles), more, powerful flares spectacularly explode, and brilliant prominences loop or erupt high above the Sun's surface.

Radiative Zone

As the photons, or light particles, rush out from the Sun's core, they pass through a thick layer of slightly cooler gas known as the radiative zone. The photons bounce around in this area like tiny balls in a giant pinball game. Each photon can travel only a fraction of a centimetre before hitting an **atom** of gas and being knocked back. No wonder it takes millions of years for light to make its way through the Sun!

Solar Eclipse

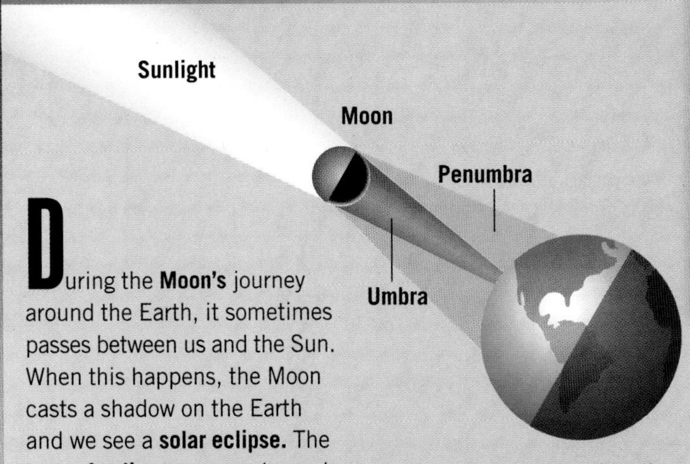

During the **Moon's** journey around the Earth, it sometimes passes between us and the Sun. When this happens, the Moon casts a shadow on the Earth and we see a **solar eclipse.** The type of **eclipse** you see depends on where you are. A partial eclipse is seen from within the Moon's penumbra (partial shadow). If you are lucky enough to be in an area covered by the Moon's umbra (main shadow), you will see a total eclipse. Only about 70 total solar eclipses occur each century.

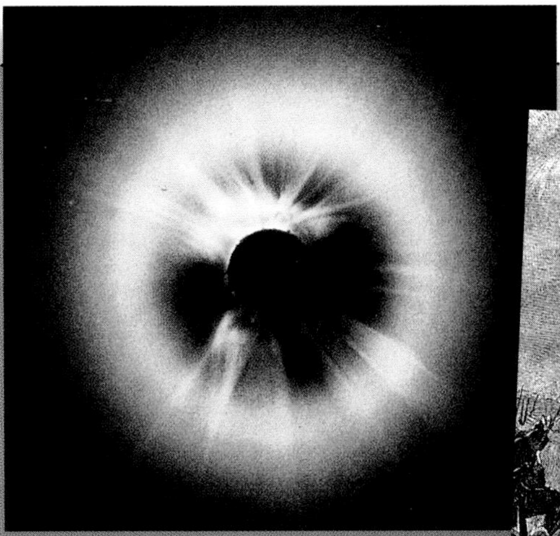

During a total eclipse, the Moon blocks the glare of the Sun's surface. That makes it possible to see prominences leaping up from the chromosphere and the wispy streamers of the **corona**—the ghostly halo of gases that makes up the Sun's outermost layer.

Labels on diagram: Sunlight, Moon, Penumbra, Umbra

Eclipse Fear

Through the ages, people have feared solar eclipses. The Chinese thought a dragon was trying to swallow the Sun. As soon as an eclipse began, they made loud noises to scare the dragon away. In 585 BC, a solar eclipse ended a five-year war between two Middle Eastern armies, the Lydians and the Medes. The eclipse occurred in the middle of a battle. When the frightened soldiers saw the Sun disappear and the sky darken, they immediately stopped fighting *(above)* and made peace.

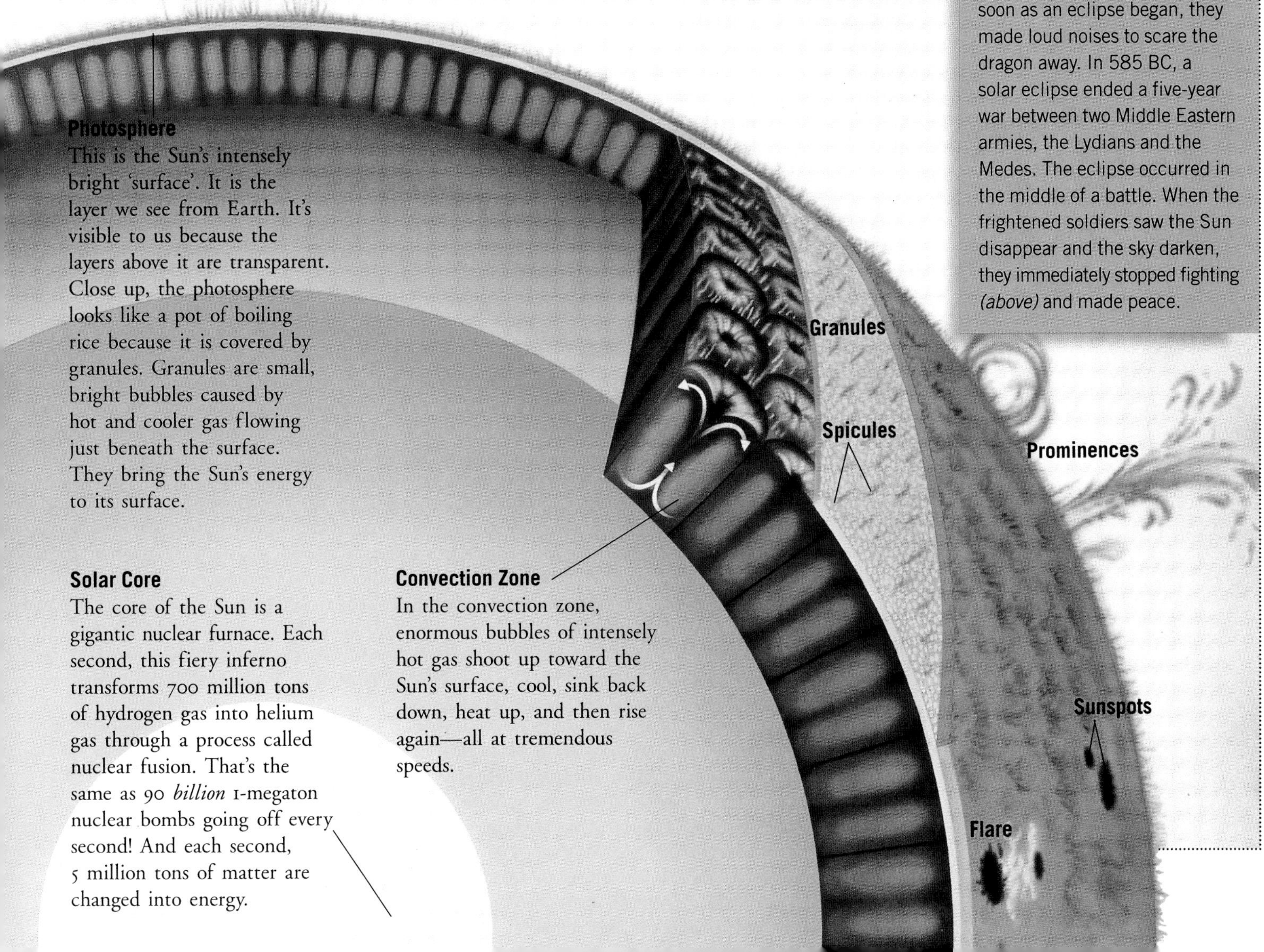

Photosphere

This is the Sun's intensely bright 'surface'. It is the layer we see from Earth. It's visible to us because the layers above it are transparent. Close up, the photosphere looks like a pot of boiling rice because it is covered by granules. Granules are small, bright bubbles caused by hot and cooler gas flowing just beneath the surface. They bring the Sun's energy to its surface.

Solar Core

The core of the Sun is a gigantic nuclear furnace. Each second, this fiery inferno transforms 700 million tons of hydrogen gas into helium gas through a process called nuclear fusion. That's the same as 90 *billion* 1-megaton nuclear bombs going off every second! And each second, 5 million tons of matter are changed into energy.

Convection Zone

In the convection zone, enormous bubbles of intensely hot gas shoot up toward the Sun's surface, cool, sink back down, heat up, and then rise again—all at tremendous speeds.

Labels on illustration: Granules, Spicules, Prominences, Sunspots, Flare

Magnetic Dynamo

Like Earth and most other planets in the **solar system,** the Sun is a gigantic magnet. It has long, invisible **magnetic field lines** that run between its north and south poles. But because the Sun is made completely of **gas** (it's not solid like Earth), it rotates in a weird way that makes its field lines behave much differently from those on Earth.

What happens is this: the Sun rotates faster at its equator (about every 27 days) than at its poles (about every 34 days). This causes the magnetic field lines to wrap around the Sun. The lines that cross the faster-moving equator are dragged ahead of the lines nearer the slower-moving poles. At the same time, the lines rise and fall along with the currents of hot gas in the Sun and are twisted and intertwined into magnetic rubber bands.

All this stretching and twisting strengthens the magnetic field. The twisted lines rise to the surface, where they form **sunspots** and release **energy** as prominences and other eruptions. Eventually, the Sun's magnetic fields weaken, causing activity on the surface to quieten down. But then the process begins again, and the magnetic activity slowly rebuilds.

As the Sun Turns

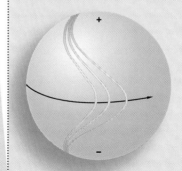

By tracking sunspots across the Sun's surface, scientists have discovered that the Sun rotates about seven days faster at its equator than at its poles. This uneven rotation strengthens the Sun's magnetic fields and causes sunspots and violent eruptions on the Sun's surface.

Magnetic Fields

each other, knotting like rubber bands being twisted *(below)*. Sometimes, loops of tangled magnetic lines pop above the Sun's surface. Like a horseshoe magnet, the loops have north and south magnetic poles at their ends.

The Sun's uneven **rotation** causes its magnetic field lines to be pulled and stretched unevenly *(above).* The lines at the Sun's equator move out ahead because the Sun rotates faster here than at its poles. As the Sun keeps rotating, the lines start to wrap around

Sun Worship

Many ancient cultures worshipped the Sun. The Egyptians called their Sun god Ra. On this 3,000-year-old gold ornament, Ra is symbolized by a blue beetle, or scarab. He is riding in a boat through the dark, evil world of the dead. The Moon god, Thoth, sits on both sides of Ra to help guide him on this dangerous journey.

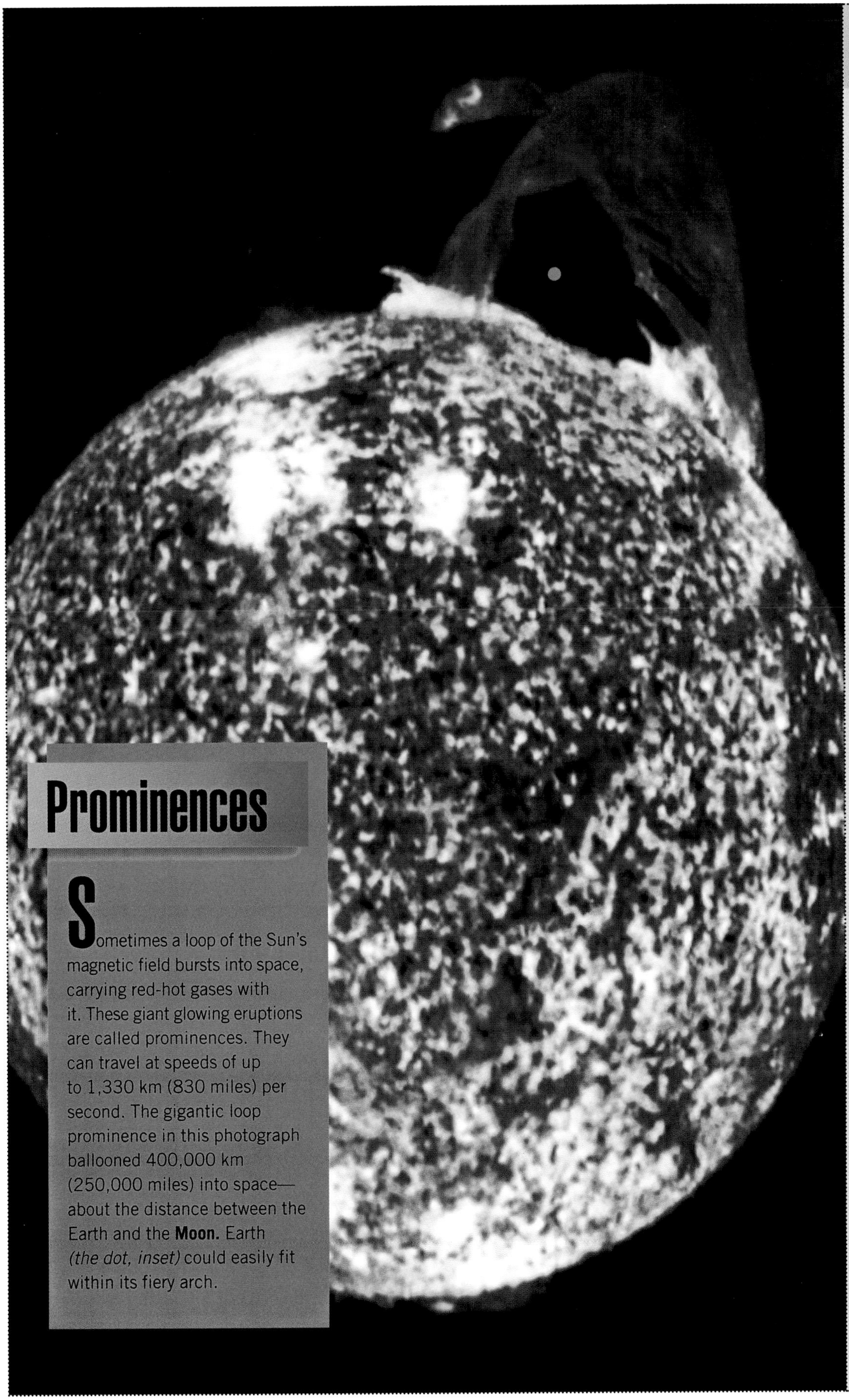

Sunspots

Sunspots—areas of cooler, darker gas on the Sun's surface—range in width from a few hundred kilometres to a whopping 80,000 km (50,000 miles)—about six times Earth's diameter. They often appear in pairs, one at each place where a loop of magnetic field protrudes from the Sun's surface. Sunspots can last for months or disappear after a day or two. The number of sunspots goes up and down in a regular cycle that lasts about 11 years. At the beginning of the cycle, known as sunspot minimum, the Sun is almost bare of spots *(below top)*. By sunspot maximum *(below bottom)*, the Sun's magnetic fields have created dozens of large spots.

Sunspot Minimum

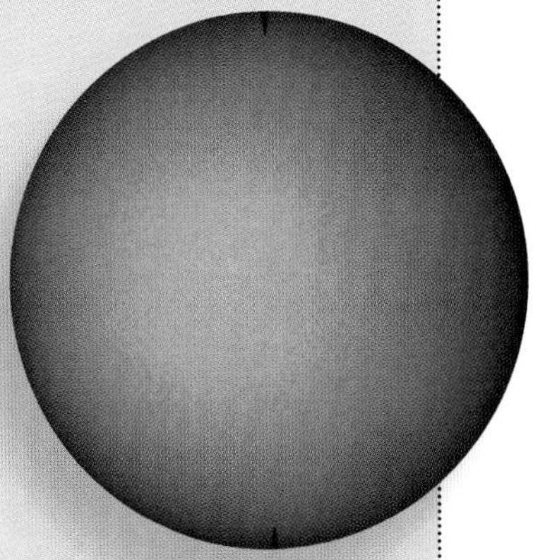

Sunspot Maximum

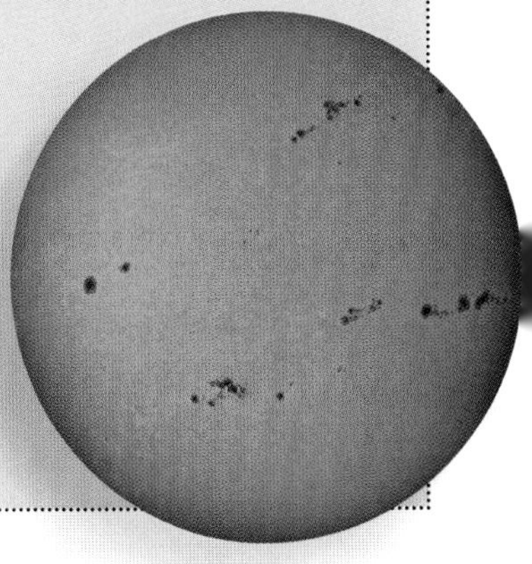

Prominences

Sometimes a loop of the Sun's magnetic field bursts into space, carrying red-hot gases with it. These giant glowing eruptions are called prominences. They can travel at speeds of up to 1,330 km (830 miles) per second. The gigantic loop prominence in this photograph ballooned 400,000 km (250,000 miles) into space—about the distance between the Earth and the **Moon**. Earth *(the dot, inset)* could easily fit within its fiery arch.

What Is the Solar Wind?

In a way, the Sun is evaporating. It is constantly losing charged **gas** particles, called **plasma**. As these particles fly into space, they form the **solar wind**. Plasma escapes from the Sun in areas where the Sun's **magnetic field lines** extend out into space rather than loop back to its surface. As these solar wind particles zoom forward through space, they build up enormous speed. The fastest winds come from gigantic holes in the **corona** (right). By the time this wind reaches Earth, it is travelling at speeds of up to 750 km (470 miles) per second!

Most solar wind goes around the Earth, diverted by our planet's magnetic field. Those solar particles that hit the **atmosphere** cause auroras (next page) and geomagnetic storms. These aren't storms you see or feel, like thunderstorms. They disrupt radio communications and interfere with the transmission of electricity from power plants.

About 1 million tons of solar plasma rush through coronal holes each second. Still, the Sun has lost less than 0.1 percent of its **mass** since it was formed 4.6 billion years ago.

Holey Corona!

The Sun looks like it has a bald spot in this photograph taken with a special x-ray camera. The bald spot is actually a hole in the corona. Plasma—the stuff the Sun is made of—escapes through these gigantic holes and shoots out into space, creating the solar wind. As the Sun rotates, so does the coronal hole, spewing particles into space much like a lighthouse beacon. When a coronal hole faces Earth, we're blasted by these particles that cause geomagnetic storms in our atmosphere.

Strange But TRUE!

A Solar Power Surge

On March 10, 1989, a series of strange events happened on Earth. Shortwave radio operators around the world suddenly lost contact with one another for 24 hours. Communication was also lost with 11,000 of the 19,000 **satellites** that were **orbiting** the Earth. In Montreal, Canada, a mysterious power surge overwhelmed the electric company, shutting off much of the city's electricity for nine hours. Elsewhere, people watched in wonder as their automatic garage doors opened and closed on their own.

What caused all these odd happenings? An extremely strong gust of solar wind. A huge burst of plasma had escaped from the Sun the day before. When the plasma reached Earth it caused a geomagnetic storm, which for a short time messed up electrical equipment and radio transmissions around the world.

A Solar Blast-off

Huge blasts of solar wind are called coronal mass ejections. They can hurl up to 100 billion tons of plasma into space at speeds of more than 500 km (300 miles) per second. These photographs, taken over a two-hour period, show a gigantic coronal mass ejection in the making.

At first, the solar wind escapes through the Sun's corona relatively quietly. The plasma, seen here as wispy streamers, is travelling along open magnetic field lines.

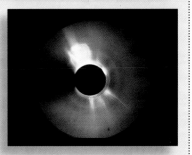

Then a large cloud of plasma breaks away from the Sun's surface. The rapidly expanding gas pushes the Sun's magnetic field lines higher and higher into the Sun's corona.

When the expanding plasma cloud gets high enough, it splits open the looped magnetic field. The plasma breaks free and is carried out into space by the solar wind like a gigantic soap bubble.

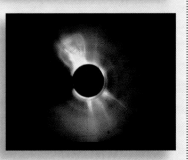

What's an Aurora?

Blaze of Colour in the Sky

When a solar wind gust reaches Earth, it creates millions of amps of electrical current. Beams of **electrons** in the current flow down Earth's magnetic field lines near its poles. When the electrons hit **atoms** and molecules in Earth's atmosphere, they make them glow in eerie colours. This glow is called an aurora. Auroras usually appear only near the poles.

Mercury the Fastest Planet

Mercury is the closest **planet** to the Sun. It's also the fastest. Like the ancient Roman messenger god it was named after *(below),* Mercury races through space, circling the Sun once every 88 days. This gives it the shortest 'year' in the **solar system.** Yet Mercury spins very slowly on its **axis**—about once every 59 days. (Earth spins once every 24 hours.) That makes for extremely odd sunsets in which the Sun zigzags across the sky for almost three Earth months before finally setting.

Mercury has the widest range of temperatures of any planet. In daytime, its surface can get as hot as 400°C (800°F)—hot enough to melt lead! At night, the temperature can dive to an ultracold -185°C (-300°F).

Mercury has a huge iron core that makes up almost three-fourths of the entire planet. The core is covered by a layer of rock. Mercury's surface is pockmarked with **craters,** which makes it look a lot like Earth's **Moon.**

Rocky Crust

Rocky Molten Mantle

Iron Core

Fast FACTS

Symbol ☿

Location First planet from the Sun

Average Distance from Sun 58 million km (36 million miles)

Rotation/Length of Day About 59 Earth days

Revolution/Length of Year 88 Earth days

Orbital Speed 172,408 km/h (107,132 mph)

Diameter 4,878 km (3,031 miles)

Axial Tilt 0°

Mass About 1/18 that of Earth

Gravity About 2/5 that of Earth; a 45-kg (100-lb.) Earthling would weigh 18 kg (40 lb.) on Mercury

Average Surface Temperature Mercury has the greatest range of any planet, with surface temperatures as cold as -185°C (-300°F) and as hot as 400°C (800°F)

Major Atmospheric Gases Extremely thin atmosphere with only small traces of oxygen

Moons None

Rings None

Like the Moon, Mercury is covered with craters because it doesn't have enough **atmosphere** to protect its surface from incoming **meteoroids, asteroids, and comets.** Almost half of its most recent craters were caused by comets smashing into its surface at nearly 85 km (53 miles) per second.

Fabulous Features!

Wrinkles

When Mercury's huge iron core cooled and shrank, it caused the planet's surface to wrinkle—like the skin of an apple wrinkles when its fleshy inside dries up. This wrinkling caused huge cliffs, or scarps, to form across Mercury's bleak surface.

Caloris Basin

Shock Waves

Hill and Valley Area

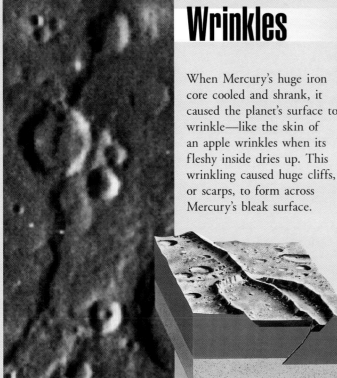

The line in the photograph at left is a portion of a big scarp that measures 500 km (300 miles) long and 2 km (1.2 miles) high. A drawing of a scarp shows it cutting across a crater—which means that the crater was there first.

Caloris Basin

One of the largest craters in the solar system is called the Caloris Basin. It was formed when a huge asteroid-sized object slammed into Mercury *(above)*. The object hit so hard that it sent powerful shock waves throughout the planet. When the waves reached the other side, they shook and shattered the surface into a roughed-up area of hills and valleys.

What's It
Like?

On Mercury

If you could stand on Mercury's cratered surface, the first thing you might notice is the eerie silence. You could throw a rock or shout, but there would be no sound. Mercury's atmosphere is too thin to carry sound.

It's also too thin to scatter light waves, so the sky always looks black, even in the daytime. The Sun, however, looks about three times bigger than it does on Earth.

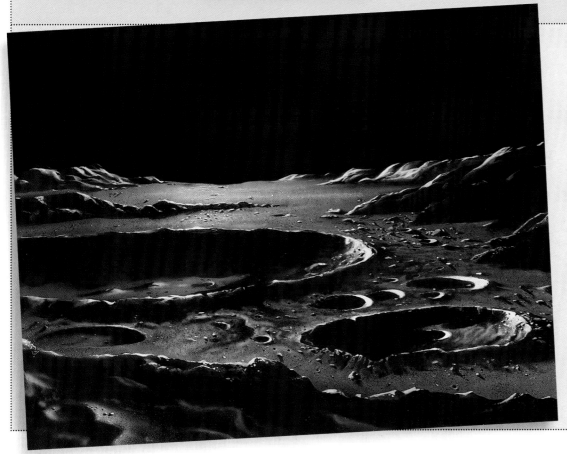

Venus Earth's Twin

Venus, the second-closest **planet** to the Sun, is sometimes called Earth's 'twin' because the two planets are so close in **density** and size. And like Earth, Venus has an **atmosphere.** But that's where the similarities end. Venus is a hot inferno of poisonous gases and crushing atmospheric pressure 90 times stronger than Earth's. When the Russian spacecraft *Venera* 14 landed there in 1982 *(right)*, it sent back photos and data for only 57 minutes before it sizzled and melted.

Venus was named after the Roman goddess of love and beauty *(below)*. From Earth, Venus does look beautiful; only the **Moon** shines brighter in the night sky. This brightness is caused by Venus's thick clouds, which reflect sunlight away from its surface. The clouds are filled with carbon dioxide and other **gases** that trap heat—a phenomenon known as the greenhouse effect. That's why temperatures on Venus never drop much below 500°C (900°F), even at night. Both days and nights are very long on Venus, for the planet rotates only once every 243 days. Yet Venus revolves around the Sun every 225 days. That makes its day longer than its year!

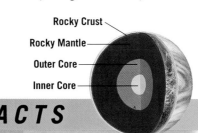

Rocky Crust
Rocky Mantle
Outer Core
Inner Core

Fast FACTS

Symbol ♀

Location Second planet from the Sun

Average Distance from Sun 108 million km (67 million miles)

Rotation/Length of Day 243 Earth days

Revolution/Length of Year 225 Earth days

Orbital Speed 126,111 km/h (78,364 mph)

Diameter 12,100 km (7,520 miles)

Axial Tilt 2.6°

Mass About $\frac{4}{5}$ that of Earth

Gravity $\frac{9}{10}$ that of Earth; a 45-kg (100-lb.) Earthling would weigh 40 kg (90 lb.) on Venus

Average Surface Temperature About 500°C (900°F)

Major Atmospheric Gases Carbon dioxide

Moons None

Rings None

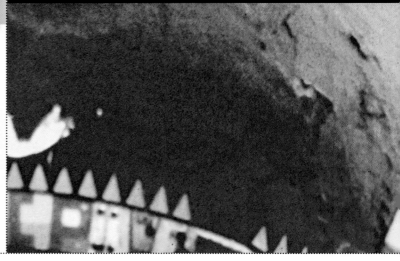

During its brief stay on Venus, *Venera 14 (above)* sent photographs like this ground view *(below)* back to Earth. The photo reveals a barren landscape with slabs of volcanic rock tossed about on grainy soil.

What's It Like?

On Venus

If you could stand on Venus, probably the first thing you would notice is the unbearable heat and pressure. The heat is great enough to turn lead to liquid. The atmospheric pressure is as great as being almost 1 kilometre under Earth's ocean.

The atmosphere is so thick that it always looks like a very cloudy day on Earth. The sky is orange and casts a fiery glow over the ground below. The thick atmosphere causes sunlight to bend, which is why the Sun looks strangely flat and oval shaped from Venus.

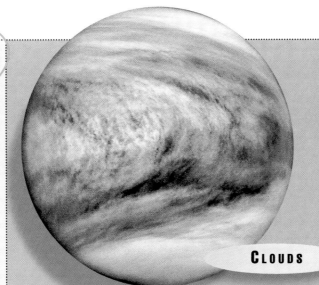

CLOUDS

Venus's upper clouds move fast. They race across the sky at speeds of about 300 km/h (200 mph)—three times as fast as most hurricanes on Earth.

SURFACE

This view of Venus was made by bouncing radar signals off its surface. It shows what Venus would look like without clouds.

TOPOGRAPHY

Colour has been added to this radar map of Venus to show the highest (*brownish red*) and lowest (*blue*) surface features. Green patches mark the areas in between.

Venus Revealed

For years, scientists looking through telescopes could not 'see' the surface of Venus, only its dense cloud cover. They thought the planet might have a humid, tropical climate, and they could only guess at what the surface looked like. Space probes have revealed Venus to be a terribly hot place—a boiling, barren desert rather than a lush jungle—and while its surface is pretty flat, it does have a few towering mountains, some as high as 6 km (4 miles).

Fabulous Features!

Spiders and Pancakes

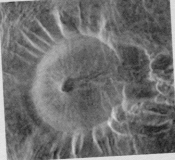

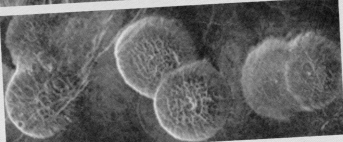

Venus is a strange place, unlike any other in the **solar system.** It is much flatter than Earth. Most of its surface is low, gently rolling plains. But Venus does have volcanoes, some with unusual shapes. One group of volcanoes has flattened, round domes—each about 25 km (16 miles) across—that look like pancakes (*below*); another has domes shaped like giant spiders (*left*). Scientists call these bizarre volcanoes 'arachnoids', meaning spider-like.

Venus has few meteorite craters. Scientists think this is because most of its original surface has been destroyed and covered up by volcanic lava. Most of Venus's surface is probably very young—about 400 million years old.

Earth the Blue Planet

Earth is the most active of the rocky **planets.** Its surface is constantly changing. The reason why can be found deep inside the planet. At its centre, Earth has a hot, solid iron inner **core.** Surrounding the core is a layer of liquid iron. Between this layer and Earth's thin crust is the **mantle**—a thick layer of rock that is so hot that it acts like melted plastic. Earth's crust is broken up into huge sheets called tectonic plates that ride on top of the gooey, elastic mantle. As these plates collide or pull apart from one another, the ground shakes, volcanoes erupt, and mountains rise up.

Earth has other unique features. It's the only planet with much liquid water, which covers two-thirds of its surface. Water is the reason why the Navajo people paint their 'Mother Earth' deity blue *(left)*. Earth also has a protective **atmosphere.** But Earth's most singular feature is the most amazing one: life.

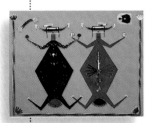

Navajo sand painting shows Mother Earth and Father Sky.

Earth is known as the Blue Planet because most of its surface is covered by blue ocean waters. From space, it looks like a colourful marble with swirls of green, brown, and white mixed in with the blue. Earth's life-giving water is constantly being recycled. Heated by the Sun, it evaporates, condenses into clouds, and then rains back onto the surface, where it starts the recycling process all over again.

Fast FACTS

Rocky Crust
Rocky Mantle
Liquid Outer Core
Solid Inner Core

Symbol ⊕

Location Third planet from the Sun

Average Distance from Sun 150 million km (93 million miles)

Rotation/Length of Day 23 hours, 56 min.

Revolution/Length of Year 365.25 days (which is why every fourth year we have to add a day to our calendar year)

Orbital Speed 107,245 km/h (66,641 mph)

Diameter 12,756 km (7,926 miles)

Axial Tilt 23.5°

Mass 6 trillion trillion kg (13 trillion trillion lb.)

Average Surface Temperature 14°C (57.2°F)

Major Atmospheric Gases Nitrogen and oxygen

Moons 1

Rings None

23.5°

Sun's Rays

A Slant on the Seasons

Like a giant spinning top, the Earth tilts at an angle as it twirls around—a 23.5° angle, to be precise. It's because of this tilt that we have seasons. As the Earth travels around the Sun, one hemisphere, or half of the planet, always leans in the direction of the Sun. The Sun's rays hit this part more directly, causing summer. Meanwhile, it is winter in the hemisphere leaning away from the Sun.

Wow! That's Change!

Pangaea

Today

Earth's surface is always changing. Only 250 million years ago, all of Earth's continents were probably joined together in one large landmass called Pangaea, which means 'all-Earth'. It gradually moved apart into the seven continents we see today. The continents continue to move. North America and Europe, for example, are moving apart at a rate of about 4 cm (1.6 in.) per year.

On Earth, even giant mountains don't last forever. Wind, water, and other forces gradually wear them down.

When Did Life Begin?

Life is a very recent event in Earth's history. Our home planet formed about 4.6 billion years ago, but it took another billion years for conditions to be right for life. Earth's first life forms were simple, single-celled organisms that appeared 3.5 billion years ago. The dinosaurs then came along about 250 million years ago. And humans are truly the planet's babies! The first modern humans—*Homo sapiens*—only emerged 200,000 years ago.

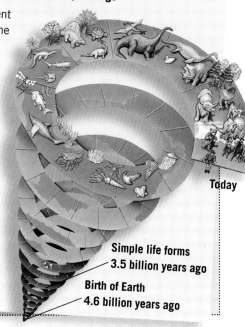

**Rise of dinosaurs
250 million years ago**

Today

**Simple life forms
3.5 billion years ago**

**Birth of Earth
4.6 billion years ago**

Moon
Earth's Satellite

The **Moon** is Earth's closest neighbour. The two have been travelling companions through space for more than four billion years. As the Moon **orbits** the Earth its **gravity** tugs on our planet, causing it to bulge out slightly. This results in the daily rise and fall of the ocean that we call high and low tides.

Unlike Earth, the Moon is a dead, hostile place. It has no **atmosphere,** and what water it has is frozen in its soil. Temperatures climb to a blistering 115ºC (240ºF) during the Moon's day and drop to a bone-chilling -160ºC (-260ºF) at night.

The Moon's surface is covered with **craters.** Most were caused by **meteoroids, asteroids,** and **comets.** A few were formed by volcanism. About 3.5 billion years ago, lava flowed up from the Moon's interior and hardened into smooth plains called maria—the dark patches we see from Earth. Although the Moon looks bright, it doesn't produce any light of its own; instead it reflects light from the Sun.

Most ancient peoples, including the Romans, worshipped the Moon. They named their Moon goddess Diana *(left)* and believed she rode a chariot across the night sky.

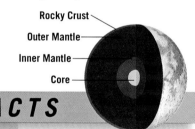

Now You See It

The near side of the Moon—the side we always see from Earth—has been studied and mapped for centuries. Early astronomers thought the dark areas were seas. Today, scientists know that they are maria, regions of cooled, hardened lava. The huge, bright crater near the bottom is called Tycho.

Now You Don't

In 1959, a Russian space probe sent back the first photographs of the far side of the Moon —the side that always faces away from Earth. Although this side of the Moon has many more craters, it has far fewer maria. Scientists think it's because the Moon's rocky crust is thicker on the far side, making it more difficult for hot lava to rise up from the Moon's interior.

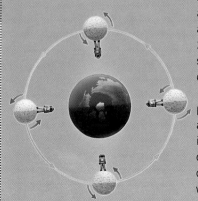

Rocky Crust
Outer Mantle
Inner Mantle
Core

Fast FACTS

Symbol ☾
Location Orbits around the Earth
Average Distance from Earth 383,000 km (238,000 miles)
Rotation/Length of Day About 27 Earth days
Orbit around Earth About 27 Earth days

Diameter 3,475 km (2,160 miles), or about ¼ that of Earth
Mass ⅛₁ that of Earth
Gravity ⅙ that of Earth; a 45-kg (100-lb.) Earthling would weigh 7 kg (17 lb.) on the Moon
Average Surface Temperature From -160ºC (-260ºF) to 115ºC (240ºF)
Major Atmospheric Gases None

Does the Moon Rotate?

Yes! But the Moon rotates very slowly. It spins once on its **axis** in exactly the same amount of time it takes to go around the Earth once—about 27 days. That's why the same side always faces Earth and the other side always faces away.

Confused? Look at the picture at left. As the Moon goes around the Earth, the astronaut is standing in the same place on the Moon's surface, but you can see the astronaut rotating with the Moon.

Phases of the Moon

Crescent	First Quarter	Gibbous	Full	Gibbous	Last Quarter	Crescent

Waxing — Waning

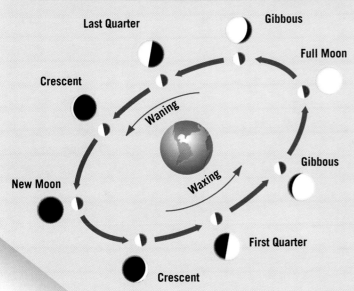

Last Quarter · Gibbous · Full Moon · Crescent · Waning · Waxing · New Moon · Gibbous · First Quarter · Crescent · Sunlight

One of the most fascinating —and predictable—sights in the night sky is the changing of the Moon's shape. About every 30 days, the Moon goes through a complete cycle of shapes, called lunar phases. Of course, the Moon doesn't really change shape. What changes is the amount of the Moon's sunlit surface that is visible from Earth.

At the beginning of the cycle (the 'new Moon' phase), none of the sunlit side can be seen. The Moon is completely dark, so it appears to be invisible in the night sky. Then gradually, over the next two weeks or so, the shape of the Moon increases from crescent, to quarter, to gibbous (meaning larger than a half Moon but smaller than a full Moon). Finally, the Moon is fully lit (the 'full Moon' phase). Then the process reverses and the Moon slowly decreases in size until it seems to disappear again—another new Moon.

When the Moon is going from new to full, it is said to be waxing, or growing bigger. When it is going from full Moon to new Moon, it is said to be waning, or growing smaller. Ancient peoples based their calendars on the Moon's changing shapes. A year came to have 12 'Moon' phases, or 'months'.

Earth's Shadow

Lunar Eclipse

A **lunar eclipse** happens when the Moon passes through Earth's shadow during its full Moon phase *(above)*. The Sun, Earth, and Moon have to be lined up. The Moon doesn't disappear completely. Stray rays of sunlight still manage to reach its surface, giving it a reddish glow *(right)*. Most months, the Moon passes above or below Earth's shadow.

How Did the Moon Form?

How the Moon came to be is still a great mystery. Many scientists believe that the Moon was formed when a planet-like body about the size of Mars slammed into Earth when the Earth was still very young *(top right)*. The collision sent a cloud of rocky debris into orbit around the Earth *(middle right)*. The debris gradually came together to form one big, rocky clump—the Moon *(bottom right)*.

Exploring the Moon

What's it like to walk on the **Moon?** Here you weigh one-sixth what you weigh on Earth (divide your Earth weight by 6), which makes walking across the surface a bit of a challenge. Because you're so light you can't just step forward and expect to move. You have to thrust yourself forward as though you are stepping into the wind. And once you get going it's sort of like bouncing on a trampoline.

Then try to stop. That's not so easy. You have to dig your heels into the ground and lean backward, and hope you don't fall. But if you do, that's OK, because it's fun. It's like falling in slow motion, and you land so gently that you don't get hurt. But you do get covered in powdery, grey moondust that smells like gunpowder.

If you get tired of walking you can always hop into your four-wheel drive lunar rover. It doesn't go very fast—about 18 km/h (11 mph)—but what a ride! You bounce and pitch across a rough surface pitted with **craters.** It feels exactly like being on a small boat in a rough sea. Watch that bump! You soar into the air, six times as high as back home on Earth.

Lost and Found

A four-leaf clover, a falcon feather, a Bible, a tiny figure of a man in a spacesuit, and this plaque *(top right)* that bears the inscription: 'Here men from the planet Earth first set foot upon the Moon July 1969, A.D. We came in peace for all mankind'—these were left on the lunar surface by astronaut tourists. They also brought back 382 kg (841 lb.) of rock and soil souvenirs, including this Moon rock *(bottom right)*.

Feet Forever

This footprint left behind by an Apollo astronaut will remain on the Moon for millions of years. That's because the Moon has no **atmosphere.** Without an atmosphere, there is no wind to erode, or wear away, the Moon's surface and erase footprints like this.

Man on the Moon

Standing in the middle of a valley, astronaut Harrison Schmitt collects small pieces of rock from an enormous boulder. He nicknamed the boulder Split Rock because it was formed from two different kinds of rock. At the right of the boulder is Schmitt's lunar rover, a golf buggy-sized vehicle that astronauts used to travel about the Moon's surface—the first moon cars!

Mars the Red Planet

Mars is the only **planet** in the night sky with a red glow. It gets its colour from the iron in its soil. To ancient peoples, however, Mars seemed shrouded in blood and fire, so they named the planet after a mythological war god, whom the Romans called Mars and the Greeks called Ares *(below)*.

Mars and Earth have many things in common, which is why Mars is sometimes called Earth's 'little brother'. Their day is almost the same length; Mars takes only 41 minutes longer to turn on its axis. Both planets have mountains, canyons, deserts, volcanoes, and polar caps. Both also have riverbeds, although the ones on Mars are now dry.

Mars has some truly enormous features. One is Olympus Mons, the largest volcano in the **solar system.** Another is the Valles Marineris, a system of canyons that runs for more than 4,800 km (3,000 miles)—about the entire width of the United States. Mars also has huge dust storms that can sweep across the entire planet and last for months.

Like Earth, Mars has an icecap covering its north pole. Cutting across its equator like a gigantic scar is a huge canyon system called Valles Marineris.

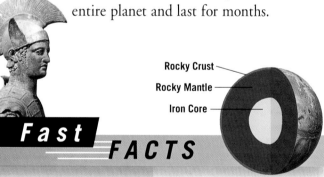

Rocky Crust
Rocky Mantle
Iron Core

Fast FACTS

Symbol ♂	**Axial Tilt** 25.2°
Location Fourth planet from the Sun	**Mass** ¹⁄₁₀ that of Earth
Average Distance from Sun 228 million km (142 million miles)	**Gravity** About ²⁄₅ that of Earth; a 45-kg (100-lb.) Earthling would weigh 18 kg (40 lb.) on Mars
Rotation/Length of Day 24 hours, 37 minutes	**Average Surface Temperature** -63°C (-81°F)
Revolution/Length of Year 687 Earth days	**Major Atmospheric Gases** Mostly carbon dioxide
Orbital Speed 86,870 km/h (53,980 mph)	**Moons** 2
Diameter 6,787 km (4,217 miles)	**Rings** None

Potato Moons

Mars has two tiny potato-shaped **moons:** Phobos and Deimos. Both were probably **asteroids** *(page 86)* that got captured by Mars's gravity.

Phobos *(top)*, the larger moon and the one closer to Mars, is 28 km (17 miles) long. It has a rocky surface with lots of **craters,** including the huge Stickney Crater, which covers about 10 percent of the moon's surface. Phobos circles the planet quickly— once every 7 hours and 39 minutes.

Deimos *(bottom)* is only 16 km (10 miles) long and has a much smoother surface. It goes around Mars about once every 30 hours.

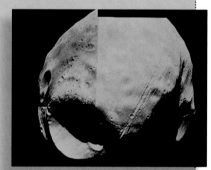

Phobos

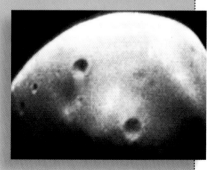

Deimos

Olympus Mons

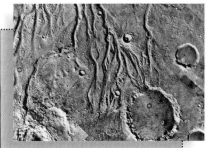

Lost Rivers

Mars has many ancient riverbeds, like those shown here. Although now dry, these channels were once filled with flowing water. Where has all that water gone? Much of it ended up in the icecap at Mars's north pole. But some of it may also lie frozen and buried deep below the Martian surface.

How **Big?**

Olympus Mons

Mount Everest

The biggest volcano in the solar system—Olympus Mons—is found on Mars. It rises 29 km (18 miles) above the Martian landscape. That makes it almost three times as tall as Earth's tallest land mountain, Mount Everest *(above)*. And when you consider how much space it takes up in all directions, it is 50 times more massive than Earth's biggest volcano—Hawaii's Mauna Loa.

Olympus Mons is extinct, which means it stopped erupting long ago. Its summit is shaped like a shield *(above, top)* with a crater that is 80 km (50 miles) wide.

Would **You** *Believe?*

'The Face'

One of the spookiest photos of Mars is this one taken by the *Viking 1* space probe in 1976. It shows what looks to be a human face rising up from a flat region of Mars known as the Plains of Cydonia. Some people thought it was a stone monument built long ago by alien beings that once lived on Mars. In 1998, the *Global Surveyor* spacecraft sent back new photos of this same area. Was there a face? No, just a group of natural rock formations that cast unusual shadows.

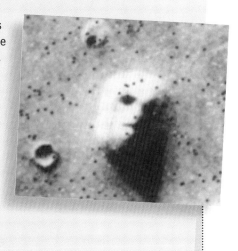

Exploring Mars

Because Mars is the **planet** most like Earth, many people have long hoped that it might be home to extraterrestrial life. In 1877, an astronomer reported seeing dark lines crisscrossing the planet, which some people thought were canals built by intelligent beings. Later, other scientists thought they saw signs of plant life.

In 1965, the American spacecraft *Mariner* 4 sent back the first closeup photos of Mars's surface. They showed a dry, barren—and apparently lifeless—planet. A decade later, two Viking landers set down on Mars to search its soil for evidence of germ-sized life called microbes. None was found. In 1997, *Pathfinder* landed on Mars. It sent out a rover, called *Sojourner (right),* which collected a wealth of information about the Martian surface and **atmosphere**—but picked up no evidence of Martian life.

Would You Believe?

In 1984, American geologist Roberta Score *(top right)* collected a fist-sized **meteorite** from Antarctica *(middle right).* Almost 10 years later, scientists figured out that it had come from Mars and contained microscopic pieces that looked like organic material—possible signs that primitive life once existed there. Among the rock's strange features is a worm-like structure, only $\frac{1}{100}$ as wide as a human hair, that looks like fossilized organisms found on Earth today *(bottom right).*

People   Percival Lowell

Lowell named 'canals' that he drew on his maps of Mars.

In 1877, a rich American businessman named Percival Lowell became fascinated with a report that an astronomer had found strange lines on the surface of Mars. Lowell immediately jumped to the conclusion that these marks were canals, dug by Martians. He thought Mars was drying out and that the Martians, in a desperate attempt to save their civilization, had built the canals to carry water from their planet's polar icecaps to arid land near its equator.

In 1894, Lowell quit his business and devoted the rest of his life to studying these Martian 'canals'. He built an observatory in Arizona, where he studied Mars night after night *(bottom right)*. He drew detailed maps *(top right)* of Mars's canals. For a time, many people shared his beliefs. But, when future space probes sent back closeup pictures of Mars, the canals were not there.

What's It *Like?*

On Mars

Be careful walking; boulders are everywhere. Hope you're not thirsty, because there's no liquid water on Mars. Look up at the sky. It's pinkish orange and the Sun looks tiny—only about half as big as back on Earth! As long as the Sun's out, though, the temperatures are comfortable. But don't take off that spacesuit! After sunset, it drops way below freezing. More importantly, you won't be able to breathe because the atmosphere here is very thin and is mostly made of carbon dioxide. The suit will also protect you from frequent dust storms. Wow! Rusty dust covers *everything*.

Imagine That!

Martians were invading America that very night! Many people panicked and fled their homes.

In 1898, the British novelist H. G. Wells wrote a book about Martians invading Earth called *The War of the Worlds*. It was full of pictures showing the menacing invaders *(right)*. Forty years later, on the eve of Halloween 1938, actor Orson Welles broadcast an updated radio version of the novel. He made it sound as if

Jupiter Gas Giant

The undisputed king of planets, Jupiter shares its name with the king of the Roman gods *(below)*. This colourful, striped beachball of a world is the biggest **planet** in the **solar system.** It is also the third-brightest light, after Venus and the Moon, in the night sky.

Jupiter is a gas giant. It has no solid surface. Instead, the planet has a small, rocky **core** surrounded by immense layers of **gas.** These layers have been squeezed so hard by the planet's powerful **gravity** that they have turned solid and liquid. An outer **atmosphere** of gas, stretching to about 70,000 km (43,000 miles) from the planet's centre, gives way to a stormy, swirling layer of clouds visible to us on Earth. Jupiter is mostly hydrogen and helium, just like the Sun. In fact, if Jupiter had been 80 times more massive, it would have built up enough heat in its core to become a **star.** Even now, the temperature at its core may reach a blistering 30,000°C (54,000°F). Because of this very hot core, Jupiter releases twice as much heat as it gets from the Sun.

On January 7, 1610, Italian mathematician Galileo Galilei turned his telescope to the night sky. Peering at Jupiter, he soon noticed what he first thought were four stars near the big planet. After watching these objects move around Jupiter, Galileo realized that they were companions of the planet, just as the Moon is Earth's companion. Galileo had discovered the first **satellites** orbiting a planet other than Earth. Today, Io, Europa, Ganymede, and Callisto are called the Galilean moons.

How Big?

Jupiter really is the Gas Giant. Jupiter is both the largest and the most massive planet in the solar system. If the **mass** of Earth is 1, then the mass of Jupiter would be 318. In fact, Jupiter's mass is about 2.5 times the mass of all the other planets in our solar system combined. All the other

The Solar System's Heavyweight Champ

planets and moons could even fit inside Jupiter. Only Saturn comes close in size, and it would occupy just more than half of Jupiter's volume. Even Jupiter's solid core has three times the volume of Earth.

Liquid Molecular Hydrogen
Liquid Metallic Hydrogen
Water
Rocky Core

Fast FACTS

Symbol ♃	**Axial Tilt** 3.08°
Location Fifth planet from the Sun	**Mass** 318 times that of Earth
Average Distance from Sun 779 million km (484 million miles)	**Gravity** 2.5 times that of Earth; a 45-kg (100-lb.) Earthling would weigh 113 kg (249 lb.) on Jupiter
Rotation/Length of Day About 10 Earth hours	
Revolution/Length of Year About 12 Earth years	**Average Temperature at Cloud Tops** -153°C (-243°F)
Orbital Speed 47,043 km/h (29,232 mph)	**Major Atmospheric Gases** Hydrogen, helium, methane
Diameter 139,822 km (86,885 miles)	**Moons** 16
	Rings 2

Jupiter's clouds swirl around the world in colourful bands. At lower left is the planet's most famous feature, the Great Red Spot, a powerful storm that has been raging for hundreds of years.

Jupiter Close up

At a distance, Jupiter's ever-changing bands, swirls, and spots look lovely, even cheerful. Yet these paint-like markings are actually huge, fierce storms and enormous banks of clouds moving through Jupiter's **atmosphere.**

The largest of these storms—in fact, the largest on any **planet** in the **solar system**—is the Great Red Spot. In many ways, the Great Red Spot is like a gigantic hurricane, with violent winds circling counterclockwise around a calm centre. It is so big that two Earths could easily fit inside it! This storm has been raging since at least 1664, when it was first seen from Earth. The smaller swirls that dot Jupiter's cloud tops are also storms, though none of these has lasted as long as the Great Red Spot.

The coloured stripes on Jupiter occur where warm **gas** rises from within the planet's atmosphere and cooler gas sinks back down, just as it does with clouds on Earth. Jupiter's rapid **rotation**—it spins on its **axis** about every 10 hours—smears these clouds into great bands.

A Stormy Weather Forecast

Zone

Jupiter's atmosphere, like that of Earth, has cooler and warmer regions that cause high and low pressure—highs and lows—that produce stormy weather across the planet's surface. On Jupiter, these are called zones and belts. The bright zones are similar to Earth's highs. They form where warm gas rises to the top of Jupiter's clouds. The dark belts are like Earth's lows, and they occur where cooler gas sinks back into Jupiter's atmosphere. Strong winds, like Earth's jet streams, flow between the zones and belts.

Splat Goes the Comet!

In July 1994, the **comet** Shoemaker-Levy 9, which had been split into fragments by Jupiter's **gravity,** made history when it became the first large object ever seen crashing into a planet. One after another, 21 chunks of comet slammed into Jupiter's atmosphere at 216,000 km/h (134,000 mph). The fragments exploded into fireballs, leaving dark blotches in Jupiter's clouds.

The Red Spot

Sometimes lighter, sometimes darker, sometimes bigger, sometimes smaller, the huge storm known as the Great Red Spot is Jupiter's most visible feature. Today, the Red Spot measures about 25,000 km (15,000 miles) by 15,000 km (9,300 miles). It spins around its centre every six days. And it has been raging for more than 300 years! The light oval just beneath it is a smaller storm that formed only 40 years ago.

What's It **Like?**

On Jupiter

Step inside the gigantic storm called the Great Red Spot (wear your best protective spacesuit). Freezing, violent winds pick you up and spin you around, flinging you through the multi-coloured clouds at close to 200 km/h (125 mph). A constant hail of ice particles, made from water, ammonia, and other chemicals, rattles against your suit. When you are tossed to the cloud tops you see the small Sun and crescent **moon** Io hovering above the horizon.

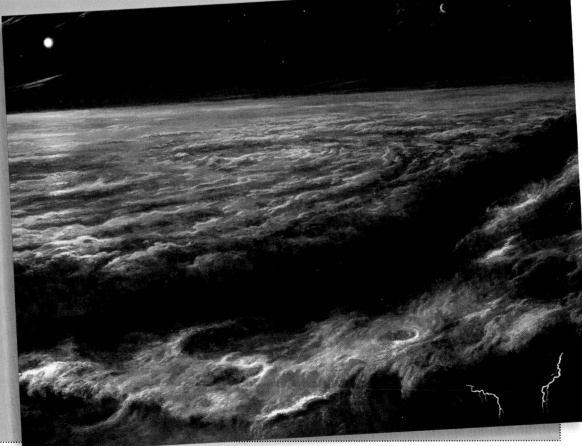

Jupiter's Moons

What Swims in Europa's Seas?

With 16 **moons,** Jupiter is like a miniature **solar system.** Its circling **satellites** spread out across more than 23 million km (14 million miles) of space. They range in size from dinky to hefty. The four that Galileo discovered—Io, Europa, Ganymede, and Callisto—are about the size of Earth's Moon. The other 12 are tiny, with Leda a mere 10 km (6 miles) in diameter: you could walk around it in four hours—if you could breathe.

The four moons Metis, Adrastea, Amalthea, and Thebe lie close to Jupiter, inside the **orbit** of Io. Scientists believe that the eight moons beyond Callisto are pieces of two large **asteroids** that Jupiter captured. Four of them—Leda, Himalia, Lysithea, and Elara—have odd orbits tilted far outside the plane of Jupiter's equator. The last four—Ananke, Carme, Pasiphae, and Sinope—are even stranger. They orbit Jupiter backward, opposite to the direction in which Jupiter rotates.

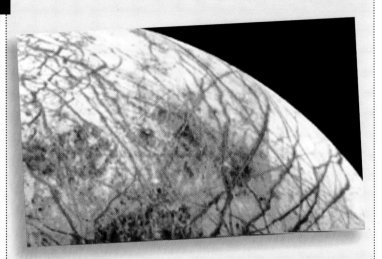

Europa has something in common with Earth: ice. The big moon's entire surface is covered with it. The lines that crisscross Europa *(above)* are cracks in the ice, caused perhaps by ice plates drifting into each other. Beneath the thick ice sheet may lie the only water ocean in the solar system aside from Earth's. If so, then some people think living organisms could swim there.

Io the Pizza Moon

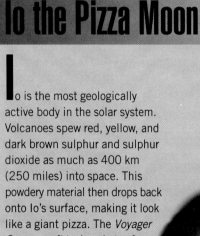

Io is the most geologically active body in the solar system. Volcanoes spew red, yellow, and dark brown sulphur and sulphur dioxide as much as 400 km (250 miles) into space. This powdery material then drops back onto Io's surface, making it look like a giant pizza. The *Voyager 2* spacecraft took a photo of one of these volcanoes erupting *(right)*. Its plume was 298 km (185 miles) high. Io also has many 'hot spots'. One of them, near Io's Loki volcano, has formed a lava lake hundreds of kilometres around.

Galilean Moons

Though similar in size, each of the four Galilean moons has its own peculiarities. Io, the one closest to Jupiter, is covered with active volcanoes. Callisto, the farthest, has more **craters** on its icy surface than any other body in the solar system. Europa, which is the smallest of the four, is covered in ice, too, but an ocean of water or slush lies beneath its surface. Ganymede, the largest, has a smooth surface marked by craters.

How Many?

Jupiter's 16 moons are mostly named for characters in mythical stories about the Roman god Jupiter. Here we show them lined up in order of closest to farthest from the planet. It's impossible to show their true sizes or distances.

Io: Fire Moon

Io, a dry, rocky ball, is covered with volcanic ash, lava, and sulpherous frost. At 3,642 km (2,263 miles) in diameter, Io is only slightly bigger than Earth's Moon. It orbits Jupiter in a little over 17.5 hours.

Europa: Ice Moon

Slightly smaller than Earth's Moon, Europa may have a deep ocean of icy slush or water beneath a layer of ice. Europa also has a thin **atmosphere** that contains water.

Ganymede: Planet Moon

Ganymede, 5,268 km (3,274 miles) in diameter, is the solar system's largest moon. In fact, it is bigger than Mercury and Pluto. Ice and movement of the moon's **crust** have erased many of Ganymede's craters.

Callisto: Crater Moon

Callisto's surface speaks of a horrendous bombardment billions of years ago. It has more craters than any other object in the solar system. Its largest crater measures about 600 km (400 miles) across.

Metis
Adrastea
Amalthea
Thebe

Io

Europa

Ganymede

Callisto

Leda
Himalia
Lysithea

Elara

Ananke
Carme
Pasiphae

Sinope

Saturn Ringed Planet

Saturn, named after the Roman god of the harvest *(below),* is the second-largest **planet** in our **solar system.** At 1.43 billion km (888 million miles) from the Sun, it is the farthest planet that you can see with the naked eye. It is also the only one whose rings can be seen through a simple telescope. Broad and bright, Saturn's spectacular rings hold billions of icy rocks in thousands of bands.

Like Jupiter, Saturn is a gas giant that gives off more **energy** than it gets from the Sun. The planet has a hot rocky **core** surrounded by liquid and solid hydrogen and helium. Its outer layer is made of **gas** and clouds. Also like Jupiter, Saturn spins at a dizzying speed, completing one **rotation** in 10.7 hours. In fact, Saturn spins so fast that it bulges around its equator. Partly because of this rapid rotation, the planet has strong winds in its **atmosphere.** They race along at up to 1,500 km/h (900 mph)—four times as fast as a tornado on Earth.

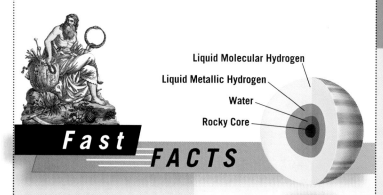

Fast FACTS

- Liquid Molecular Hydrogen
- Liquid Metallic Hydrogen
- Water
- Rocky Core

Symbol ♄

Location Sixth planet from the Sun

Average Distance from Sun 1.43 billion km (888 million miles)

Rotation/Length of Day About 11 Earth hours

Revolution/Length of Year About 29 Earth years

Orbital Speed 34,703 km/h (21,564 mph)

Diameter 116,464 km (72,371 miles)

Axial Tilt 26.7°

Mass 95 times that of Earth

Gravity 1.1 times that of Earth; a 45-kg (100-lb.) Earthling would weigh 50 kg (110 lb.) on Saturn

Average Temperature at Cloud Tops -185°C (-300°F)

Major Atmospheric Gases Hydrogen, helium, methane

Moons 18

Rings 7 major bands containing thousands of ringlets

The Mystery of Saturn's Ears

When Italian astronomer Galileo Galilei first looked at Saturn through a telescope in 1610, he drew what he saw: three round objects in a row. Having already discovered moons **orbiting** Jupiter, Galileo thought that the two ear-like circles were **moons** or **stars.** He was wrong, and his later drawings hinted at the truth. The mystery of Saturn's ears was not solved, though, until 1655. In that year, Dutch astronomer Christiaan Huygens built an improved telescope. He saw that Saturn's odd companions were really rings.

What's It *Like?*

Flying through Saturn's Rings

From Earth, Saturn's rings look smooth and solid. Up close, you would see that the rings are actually billions of glittering ice chunks. Some chunks are as big as a house. Most are smaller than a desk, looking like loosely packed dirty snowballs. It wouldn't take long for your spaceship to pierce through these icy rings. They are surprisingly thin, some only about 100 m (300 ft.) thick—the size of a football pitch. Between them are occasional dark gaps carved out by little moons.

Would **You** *Believe?*

Saturn Could Float

If you could find an ocean big enough to hold Saturn, the planet would float in it! That's because Saturn is made mostly of hydrogen and helium, both very light gases, so the planet is less dense than water (it has less **mass** for the same volume).

Saturn's Rings

How thin are Saturn's rings? They are so thin compared with their width that if a scale model were built that was 13 km (8 miles) wide, they would be only as thick as a compact disk. Unlike a CD, though, Saturn's rings are not solid. Instead they are made of billions of bits of icy debris. This space gravel may have been left over from when Saturn formed, or it may be the remains of **asteroids** or small **moons** that were torn apart by the planet's **tidal forces**—the effects of its **gravity** pulling on them. Each piece travels around Saturn in its own **orbit,** jostling other bits. Tiny moonlets in the rings sweep some areas clear of debris, producing the smaller gaps that you can see in the rings. Scientists believe that the gravitational force of Saturn's moon Mimas creates the largest gap, known as the Cassini division.

How 1 2 3 Many?

In 1675 astronomer Giovanni Cassini saw two rings. By the 20th century, there were five, the number that we can observe from Earth. Then there were thousands, seen for the first time in photographs such as this one sent to Earth by *Voyager 2*. Here the rings have been coloured by a computer to show different chemicals inside them.

Why Does Saturn Have Rings?

No one knows for sure why Saturn has so many rings. But there are a number of theories, one of which is illustrated below. The best explanations involve the Roche limit, named after the French mathematician Édouard Roche. The Roche limit is an imaginary boundary *(blue)* around Saturn. Inside this boundary moons can't form; outside it they can. Saturn's gravity is stronger than the gravitational attraction of orbiting particles. This keeps the particles apart so they are not able to clump together to grow into moons. All of Saturn's rings lie within the Roche limit, which is 144,000 km (89,500 miles) from the **planet.**

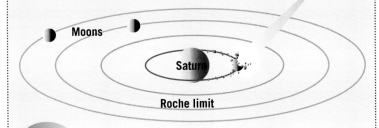

1

When Saturn was forming 4.6 billion years ago along with the rest of the planets in the **solar system,** some moons formed close to the planet—outside what was then the Roche limit. As the planet grew, the Roche limit expanded to include the moon. Later in Saturn's history, a passing **comet** or **meteoroid** collided with one of these moons and smashed it into billions of pieces *(above).*

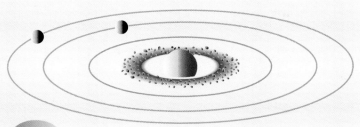

2

The pieces from the shattered moon spread out into a doughnut-shaped disk around the planet. Forces inside the Roche limit prevented the fragments from coming back together. As the particles sped round and round the planet they sometimes bumped into one another, breaking up into even smaller pieces. Eventually, these moon fragments formed the beautiful bands we see around Saturn today.

Rings, Braids, and Waves

Braided Ring

Shepherd Moons

Ring in Gap

Density Waves

Moon in Gap

Corrugation Waves

Saturn's rings are amazingly complex. From Earth they look like a few broad, colourful bands. In fact, Saturn owns thousands of rings separated by dark gaps.

With the help of Saturn's moons, some of the rings clump together into 'density waves'. As particles in the rings race past a moon, they are pulled toward it.

After many such passes, the particles bunch together into compact rings flanked by emptier spaces.

A few of Saturn's rings look like corrugated cardboard. 'Corrugation waves' form when the rings are influenced by a moon orbiting at an angle to the rings. The moon tugs the particles into orbits slightly above or below their normal

paths, producing a rippled wave.

The gaps in Saturn's rings are filled with tiny rings or moonlets that are invisible from Earth. The tiny rings are created when moonlets on either side confine the particles to a narrow band. One of Saturn's rings is a braided ring, twisted that way by two 'shepherd moons' that orbit on either side of it.

People Giovanni Cassini

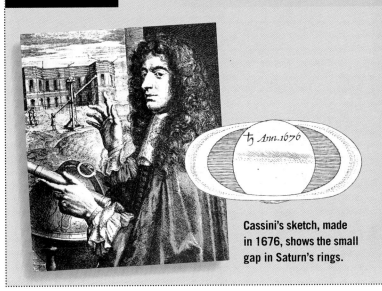

Cassini's sketch, made in 1676, shows the small gap in Saturn's rings.

In 1675, Italian-born French astronomer Giovanni Cassini discovered that Saturn's ring was actually rings, plural. A small gap separated the outer A ring from the inner B ring. In honour of that discovery, astronomers named the gap the Cassini division. Until then, scientists of the time had assumed that Saturn's ring was solid or liquid, but Cassini's discovery cast doubt on that

theory. As the first director of the Paris Observatory, Cassini worked tirelessly to build the best observatory possible using every new invention. His persistence paid off, for he used the equipment to discover four new moons around Saturn. When he lost his eyesight later in life, his son took over his duties at the observatory. In fact, Cassinis ran the Paris Observatory for 120 years.

Saturn's Moons

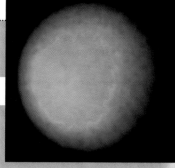

Titan

Odd Companions

When it comes to **moons,** Saturn takes the prize. It has 18 moons, more than any other **planet** in the **solar system.** And it may have others that we haven't seen yet. Pan is the smallest moon—a mere 19 km (12 miles) in diameter—as well as the closest. Phoebe, the most distant moon, is probably a captured **asteroid** or **comet.** It is the only one of Saturn's moons that does not travel in the same direction as the planet rotates. Titan, the largest of Saturn's companions, is the second-biggest moon in the solar system. It measures 5,150 km (3,200 miles) across. Titan is also the only one with a thick **atmosphere.** In fact, Titan's atmosphere is thicker than Earth's. It has many of the chemicals found in smoggy city air.

Two of the solar system's more unusual moons are Janus and Epimetheus, which share an **orbit** inside Saturn's rings. At any moment, one of the two moons has a slightly smaller orbit and travels slightly faster than its partner. Once every four years, the faster moon catches up to the slower one. When it does, the two moons change orbits and the chase begins again.

Saturn's 18 moons have an incredible variety of features. Titan *(top right),* Saturn's largest moon, is covered by a thick stew of nitrogen- and hydrocarbon-rich smog that gives it an orange glow. It also hides the moon's surface from sight. Mimas *(middle right)* is scarred by an enormous **crater,** named Herschel. The impact that made Herschel must have come close to shattering the small moon. The tug of Mimas's **gravity** may be responsible for the lack of material in the Cassini division. Iapetus *(bottom right)* has two faces— one light and one dark. Its light side always faces forward into its orbit. Its dark side always looks backward.

Mimas

Iapetus

Shepherd Moons

Tiny Prometheus and Pandora play an unusual role. They act as shepherds to keep the particles in Saturn's twisted braided ring from wandering away. The two moons orbit about 1,000 km (600 miles) on either side of the ring. Though small—each moon is about 100 to 150 km (60 to 90 miles) across—their gravitational pull is enough to nudge any stray particles back into the ring's orbit.

Saturn has 18 moons. The closest moon orbits 133,583 km (83,008 miles) from Saturn's centre, while the farthest lies about 13 million km (8 million miles) out. Their positions are shown in the drawing below, but it's impossible to show their true sizes and distances.

Pan
Atlas
Prometheus
Pandora
Janus
Epimetheus
Mimas

Enceladus

Tethys
Telesto
Calypso
Dione
Helene

Rhea

Titan

Hyperion

Iapetus

Phoebe

What's It Like?

On Titan

If you could parachute onto Titan, you would see a moon that looked like a planet. You might drop through a freezing rain of organic chemicals toward cold oceans of liquid methane and ethane. Icy islands would poke out through the polluted seas. Dim sunlight might filter through the reddish brown haze of the atmosphere.

Despite this unappealing possibility, scientists hope to learn more about Titan when the *Cassini* spacecraft arrives at Saturn in 2004 and drops the *Huygens* probe *(above)* into Titan's atmosphere. Instruments on board the probe will survey the atmosphere and take pictures of Titan's surface.

Uranus Sideways Planet

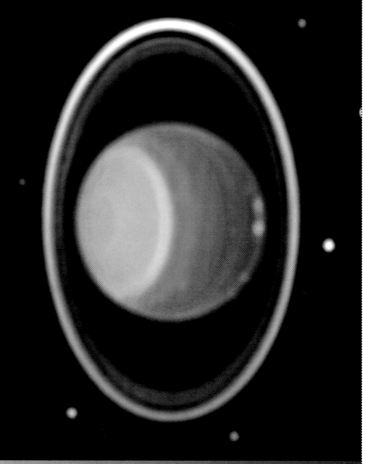

Looking at a photo of Uranus taken by the Hubble Space Telescope *(right)*, you might think that the picture was turned sideways. The picture is fine, though. It's the **planet,** its rings, and its **moons** that are flipped on their sides. No one is sure why Uranus is tilted like this. It may have smashed into an Earth-sized object early in its history. This could have knocked it on its side and chipped off the debris that formed its moons and rings.

Uranus's seasons are odd as a result of this tilt. One pole of the planet points directly at the Sun during that pole's midsummer. Forty-two Earth years later—half a year for Uranus—the other pole points at the Sun. On Uranus it is warmer at the poles than at the equator!

Uranus, a gas giant, is the third-largest planet in our **solar system.** It is named after the Roman god of the heavens *(below)*. Methane in the planet's **atmosphere** gives it its blue green colour. Much of the planet's interior is liquid or a hot, slushy mixture of water, methane, hydrogen, and helium around a rocky **core.**

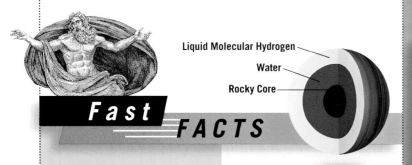

Liquid Molecular Hydrogen
Water
Rocky Core

Fast FACTS

Symbol ♅	**Axial Tilt** 97.9°
Location Seventh planet from the Sun	**Mass** 14.5 times that of Earth
Average Distance from Sun 2.86 billion km (1.78 billion miles)	**Gravity** 9/10 that of Earth; a 45-kg (100-lb.) Earthling would weigh 41 kg (90 lb.) on Uranus
Rotation/Length of Day About 17 Earth hours	**Average Temperature at Cloud Tops** -214°C (-353°F)
Revolution/Length of Year About 84 Earth years	**Major Atmospheric Gases** Hydrogen, helium, methane
Orbital Speed 24,506 km/h (15,228 mph)	**Moons** 17
Diameter 50,724 km (31,520 miles)	**Rings** 11

Mishmash Moon

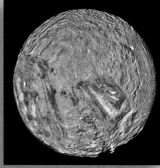

Miranda, Uranus's fifth-largest moon, has a surface unlike that of any other moon or planet in our solar system. Lightly **cratered** areas, like those of our Moon, sit next to huge grooved places called coronae. No one knows what produced such a varied landscape. Some scientists believe that a big object may have smashed into the moon, shattering it into smaller pieces. When the pieces were drawn back together by the moon's **gravity** it was left with the jumbled, mishmashed appearance it has today.

People — William Herschel

Imagine building a large telescope in your garden, pointing it to the heavens, and discovering a planet! That's what William Herschel did in 1781 when he caught sight of Uranus. He became the first person in recorded history to discover a planet. Herschel was a musician and avid amateur astronomer. He and his sister Caroline *(right)* had a number of astronomical discoveries to their credit. In 1782, Herschel was appointed King's Astronomer by George III. He made many more important discoveries during his life.

Uranus has 17 small moons, all less than 1,600 km (1,000 miles) wide. Most are named after characters in the plays of William Shakespeare. This drawing shows their locations, but it's impossible to show their true sizes and distances.

What's It Like? — On Miranda

Travelling across Miranda, Uranus's 11th moon, would be no picnic. The little world is barren and icy. It has no atmosphere. The ground is rough and jagged. Huge ridges and valleys lead to giant cliffs twice the height of Mount Everest. In the moon's dark sky, Uranus would glow, huge and blue green against a background of glittering **stars.**

Cordelia
Ophelia

Bianca
Cressida
Desdemona
Juliet
Portia
Rosalind
Belinda
Puck

Miranda

Ariel

Umbriel

Titania

Oberon

S/1997 U2

S/1997 U1

Neptune Windy Planet

Neptune is the coldest of the giant gas planets. It is also the windiest planet in the **solar system.** Along its equator, Neptune's winds race eastward at speeds greater than 2,000 km/h (1,200 mph). Like Jupiter and Saturn, Neptune gives off more heat than it gets from the Sun. Heat rising from within the **planet** moves through the **atmosphere** in currents. The currents are twisted by Neptune's rapid spin, creating strong winds.

Neptune's winds power enormous storms. Pictures taken by the *Voyager* 2 spacecraft found four large oval storms. The biggest, named the Great Dark Spot, is accompanied by a bright cloud feature, nicknamed Scooter. Wispy clouds, looking like Earth's cirrus clouds, change rapidly on Neptune, forming and disappearing over several hours. *Voyager* 2 also proved that Neptune has four dusty rings that are much thicker in some places than in others.

Because the planet's blue colour reminds people of the sea, it was named after the Roman god of the sea *(left)*.

Freezing clouds, tinted by methane, give Neptune its blue colour. You can see the Great Dark Spot, bigger than Earth, on the equator, and the Small Dark Spot, lower right.

Liquid Molecular Hydrogen

Water

Rocky Core

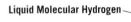

Fast FACTS

Symbol Ψ	**Axial Tilt** 28.8°
Location Eighth planet from the Sun	**Mass** 17.1 times that of Earth
Average Distance from Sun 4.49 billion km (2.79 billion miles)	**Gravity** 1.1 times that of Earth; a 45-kg (100-lb.) Earthling would weigh 50 kg (110 lb.) on Neptune
Rotation/Length of Day About 16 Earth hours	**Average Temperature at Cloud Tops** -225°C (-373°F)
Revolution/Length of Year About 164 Earth years	**Major Atmospheric Gases** Hydrogen, helium, methane
Orbital Speed 19,524 km/h (12,132 mph)	**Moons** 8
Diameter 49,526 km (30,775 miles)	**Rings** 4

Numbers Don't Lie

After Uranus's discovery, astronomers noted that its **orbit** was not what was predicted by the laws of physics. In 1845, John Couch Adams *(left)*, then a university student in England, and Urbain Leverrier *(right)*, a French astronomer, calculated that Uranus's **orbit** was affected by the gravita-

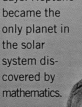

tional pull of an undiscovered eighth planet. The two even figured out where to find the mystery planet. Using Leverrier's numbers, German astronomer Johann Galle found Neptune in two days. Neptune became the only planet in the solar system discovered by mathematics.

Captured Moon Zooms Backward

Triton is a giant of a **moon,** the largest body in the solar system to orbit backward. Its path around Neptune is also tilted relative to the planet's equator. Astronomers considering these facts conclude that Triton is a captured small planet. Triton will slowly spiral inward on its backward orbit, dooming it to crash into Neptune within the next 100 million years.

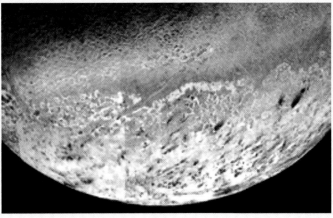

Triton's active geology may have wiped out any large impact craters.

Except for Triton, Neptune's eight moons are relatively small. Nereid has a very weird orbit that brings it as close as 1.4 million km (870,000 miles) to Neptune and takes it as far as 9.6 million km (5.9 million miles) away from the planet.

Naiad
Thalassa
Despina
Galatea
Larissa

Proteus

Triton

Nereid

What's It Like?

On Triton

Put on your extra-thick space-suit. At -235°C (-391°F), the surface of Triton is the coldest ground in the solar system. Without protective clothing you would be freeze-dried instantly! Nitrogen and methane ice cover everything, giving the moon a blue tint where the ice is fresh and a red colour where it is old.

Huge geysers spew nitrogen, ice, and carbon compounds high into Triton's thin atmosphere. In this picture, you can see a wind-blown geyser plume stretching along the horizon. Enormous frozen lakes and wrinkled terrain would make a journey across Triton difficult.

Pluto Ice Planet

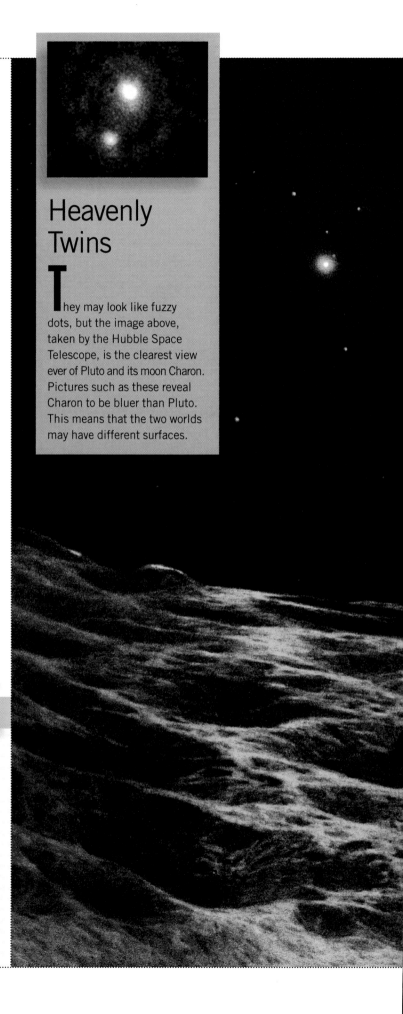

We know little about Pluto, the only **planet** discovered in the 20th century and the only one not yet visited by a space probe. What we do know is that Pluto is small, about the size of our Moon. Scientists believe it has a thin, frigid **atmosphere** of methane and nitrogen that is slowly escaping into space. When Pluto reaches its closest point to the Sun, the atmosphere is **gas.** When the planet's **orbit** takes it away from the Sun, the gas freezes into a snowy layer on the planet's surface. We also know that Pluto's poles are tipped nearly 99 degrees relative to its orbit. Because Pluto is such a forbidding world, it takes its name from the Roman god of the dead *(below).*

In 1978, astronomer James Christy of the U.S. Naval Observatory discovered that Pluto has a moon. Charon is half the size of Pluto, and it orbits very close to the planet. Charon's orbit is tilted so steeply that it swings above and below Pluto's orbit around the Sun. Astronomers sometimes think of these two small companions as a double planet.

Heavenly Twins

They may look like fuzzy dots, but the image above, taken by the Hubble Space Telescope, is the clearest view ever of Pluto and its moon Charon. Pictures such as these reveal Charon to be bluer than Pluto. This means that the two worlds may have different surfaces.

Water and Methane Ice

Rocky Core

Fast FACTS

Symbol ♇

Location Ninth planet from the Sun

Average Distance from Sun 5.91 billion km (3.67 billion miles)

Rotation/Length of Day About 6 Earth days

Revolution/Length of Year About 248 Earth years

Orbital Speed 17,091 km/h (10,620 mph)

Diameter About 2,274 km (1,413 miles)

Axial Tilt 98.8°

Mass Earth's mass is 454 times as great as that of Pluto

Gravity $\frac{7}{100}$ that of Earth; a 45-kg (100-lb.) Earthling would weigh 3 kg (7 lb.) on Pluto

Average Surface Temperature Probably between -228° and -238°C (-378° and -396°F)

Major Atmospheric Gases Perhaps methane, nitrogen

Moons 1

Rings 0

Pluto's Eccentric Orbit

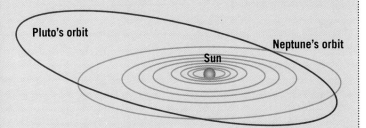

Pluto's orbit

Neptune's orbit

Sun

Of all the planets, Pluto has the most eccentric (off-centre) orbit. It curves in to within 4.3 billion km (2.7 billion miles) of the Sun and then swings out nearly 7.7 billion km (4.8 billion miles) away.

For 20 years out of each 248, Pluto's orbit lies inside Neptune's. This last occurred from 1979 to 1999. Pluto's tilted path also takes it far above the other planets when it is farthest from the Sun.

People | Clyde Tombaugh

Clyde Tombaugh discovered Pluto.

Observatory hired 22-year-old amateur astronomer Clyde Tombaugh to look for the mystery planet. In February 1930, after examining hundreds of stars in photos taken six days apart, he spotted a tiny speck of light that had moved. The planet was named Pluto, based on a suggestion by 11-year-old Venetia Burney. Though Tombaugh found Pluto near where Lowell predicted, we now know that Pluto's **gravity** is too small to have affected Uranus and Neptune.

The search began in 1905. American astronomer Percival Lowell calculated that the **solar system** must contain a ninth planet, a 'Planet X'. The gravitational pull of this unknown planet would explain what were seen as irregularities in the orbits of Uranus and Neptune. Lowell looked hard for Planet X but died in 1916, unsuccessful. Thirteen years later, the Lowell

Venetia Burney named Pluto.

What's It Like?

On Charon

To a visitor from sunny Earth, Charon would seem unfriendly indeed. Though no one has seen Charon's surface, scientists believe it is a desolate world covered with hills of water ice. One side of the moon always faces Pluto, which hangs in the starry sky like a frozen twin. At this distance from the Sun, very little warmth reaches Charon. The Sun looks like little more than a bright, faraway **star**. With so little sunlight making it to this frozen little world, it is always night on Charon.

Asteroids Minor Planets

Some 200 years ago, astronomers began searching for a 'missing planet' between Mars and Jupiter. To their amazement, they found not one big planet, but countless rocks—some large, some tiny—orbiting the Sun. They called these minor planets **'asteroids'**, which means 'star-like' in Greek.

Ceres *(below)* was the first—and biggest—asteroid to be discovered. It is 913 km (567 miles) across. Scientists believe there are more than one million asteroids, but most are too small to be seen from Earth. In fact, if you lumped all of them together into one big asteroid, its total mass would be less than that of the **Moon!**

Like bumper cars, asteroids frequently collide with one another as they speed around the Sun. They break into smaller pieces or can join together into strange shapes. Sometimes chips from these collisions are hurled toward Earth, where they can land as **meteorites.**

Types of Asteroids

Asteroids are not all alike. Some are made up of rock similar to the kinds of rocks you find on Earth. Others contain a lot of carbon—the same stuff your pencil lead is made of—which makes them very dark. Other kinds of asteroids are made mostly of nickel and iron. Some are a combination of all these materials. Scientists have divided asteroids into about a dozen different types. The three main ones are described below.

Davida

C-type

Blackish C-type asteroids contain a lot of carbon. These are the darkest asteroids because carbon does not reflect sunlight very well. Most asteroids, including Davida *(left)*, are C-types. They are found in the outer region of the **asteroid belt.**

Psyche

M-type

M-type asteroids, such as Psyche *(left)*, are made of nickel and iron. Often silvery grey, they are found mostly in the middle region of the asteroid belt. They are the brightest asteroids because they reflect sunlight so well. M-types are the least common of these three.

Eunomia

S-type

Reddish S-type asteroids contain a rocky material called silicate, which is similar to beach sand. Most S-types, such as Eunomia *(left)*, dwell in the inner region of the asteroid belt.

People Giuseppi Piazzi

On the first of January in 1801, Italian astronomer Giuseppi Piazzi *(right)* turned his telescope toward the constellation Taurus. Suddenly, he noticed a light that was not on his star chart. By the next evening the light had moved! At first he thought it was a **comet.** But after watching it for three weeks, he thought he might have found the 'lost planet' believed to exist between Mars and Jupiter. There is no such planet. Instead, Piazzi had discovered the first asteroid. He called it Ceres *(left)*, after the Roman goddess of agriculture.

Asteroid Neighbourhoods

Trojans

Amors

Atens

Asteroid Belt

Apollos

Trojans

Most asteroids are found in a region between Mars and Jupiter called the asteroid belt. They all travel in the same direction as the planets, taking three to six Earth years to make one **orbit** around the Sun. Some asteroids, however, exist outside the main belt. Two clusters, known as the Trojans, share the same orbit as Jupiter. Another group, the Amors, cross the orbit of Mars. Then there are those we have to worry about, the so-called near-Earth asteroids. Called Apollos and Atens, they have very **elliptical** orbits that cross Earth's orbit—bringing them very close to Earth. But, don't worry! There are very few of these asteroids, and one crashes into Earth only about every 500,000 years.

Imagine That!

How would you like to have an asteroid named after you? Many asteroids are named after people, including rock stars such as Jerry Garcia and Ringo Starr. There is even an asteroid named Mr Spock, after the *Star Trek* character. French author Antoine de Saint-Exupéry has an asteroid named in his honour because he created one of the most famous asteroids. In his book *The Little Prince,* the main character lives on Asteroid B-612 *(below).* Asteroids are given a permanent number and name after scientists understand them well enough to predict their orbits.

Would You Believe?

An Asteroid with Its Own Moon

When the space probe *Galileo* flew by the potato-shaped asteroid Ida in August 1993, it made an astounding discovery: Ida had its own moon! Scientists named the moon Dactyl after the Dactyls, a group of spirits in Greek mythology who live on Mount Ida on the island of Crete. Scientists think other asteroids may have moons as well.

Comets Dirty Snowballs

Kuiper Belt

Oort Cloud

With their long, glowing tails streaking across the night sky, **comets** can look spectacular. But they are nothing more than chunks of ice and dust that have earned the nickname 'dirty snowballs'. Most come from the farthest, coldest reaches of the **solar system.** They were thrown there by the **gravity** of the giant gas **planets** when the solar system was being formed.

Every once in a while, comets swing back toward the Sun. As a comet nears the Sun, it begins to heat up and vapourize, releasing **gas** and **dust** that is swept back into an extremely long tail. Many comets have tails that stretch for millions of kilometres!

Comets that come into the inner solar system travel around the Sun in **elliptical orbits.** Some swing around the Sun every 3 to 200 years. Others have orbits that bring them close to the Sun—and Earth—only once in hundreds, thousands, or even millions of years.

Home of the Comets

Comets are the long-distance runners of the solar system. Ones seen from Earth have travelled huge distances. Some begin their trip in the **Kuiper belt,** an area just beyond Neptune that is on the same flat plane as the planets. But most comets come from the **Oort cloud,** an icy, spherical region at the very edge of the solar system. Every million years or so gravity from a passing star bumps many comets in the Oort cloud out of their orbits. Some are knocked right out of the solar system; others get launched towards the Sun.

People — Edmond Halley

The most famous of all comets is Halley's comet. It is named after the British astronomer Edmond Halley *(below)*. In 1695, Halley figured out that three comets that had blazed across Earth's skies in 1531, 1607, and 1682 were actually the same object. Halley predicted

that the comet would reappear in December 1758. It did, but Halley did not live to see his prediction come true; he died in 1742. Scientists later named the comet in his honour.

Halley's comet last passed Earth in 1986 *(above)*. It will return again in 2062. By carefully studying historic records, astronomers believe Halley's comet has brightened Earth's sky about every 76 years since at least 240 BC.

Strange But TRUE!

Bad Omens

For centuries, people dreaded the sudden appearance of a comet. To them, it could only mean a bad event was about to happen. In 1472, for example, Germans blamed several terrible events—a drought, a war, and a deadly plague—on a pair of comets *(left)*. The defeat of Attila the Hun, Julius Caesar's assassination, and the downfall of Montezuma were also linked to comet appearances.

Hale-Bopp

The 1997 Comet Hale-Bopp was discovered two years earlier by American astronomer Alan Hale and amateur astronomer Thomas Bopp. It was a very bright comet even though it got no closer to Earth than about 190 million km (120 million miles). We won't see Hale-Bopp again for another 2,380 years.

Name?

Dirty Snowball

In 1950 American astronomer Fred Whipple *(below)* was the first to describe a comet as a 'dirty snowball'. His research showed that a comet is nothing more than a huge mass of ice embedded with dust. It took 36 years—and a space probe to Halley's comet—for Whipple's theory to be proved correct.

Using a clump of crushed ice and charcoal, Fred Whipple shows university students what a real comet might look like.

Comets Close up

Ion Tail

Dust Tail

A Comet's Amazing Journey

Most of a **comet's** life is spent as a drab chunk of dirty ice travelling in the outer **solar system** beyond the **orbit** of Neptune. But when it passes through the inner solar system it transforms into a beautiful, glowing object.

After an inbound comet passes the orbit of Jupiter, heat from the Sun turns some of its ice to **gas.** This gas, along with particles of **dust,** shoots out of the comet in jets.

As the comet gets closer to the Sun, the gas and dust form a huge coma, a glowing halo that surrounds the chunk of dirty ice. The chunk of ice now forms the **nucleus,** or centre, of the comet.

When the **solar wind** *(page 52)* hits gas particles in the comet, **charged particles** called **ions** are created. These ions are swept back to form an ion tail, one of the comet's two tails. The second tail, called a dust tail, is formed by the dust particles spewing out of the comet's nucleus.

Though a comet's nucleus may be no more than a few kilometres wide, its coma can be up to 1 million km (600,000 miles) across and its tail sometimes stretches for 100 million km (60 million miles), almost the distance between Venus and the Sun.

Each time a comet passes close to the Sun it loses some of its **mass.** Eventually so much is gone that it no longer glows and it becomes just a small, dark **asteroid.**

A Comet's Icy Heart

In 1986, the European space probe *Giotto* sent back pictures of Halley's comet, giving scientists the closest look ever at a comet's nucleus *(above, left)*. Halley's nucleus is a peanut-shaped lump about 16 km (10 miles) long and 8 km (5 miles) wide. On the side facing the Sun, bright jets of dust and gas shoot out from cracks in its surface. A computerized re-creation of Halley's nucleus *(above, right)* shows how it would look stripped of its gas and dust. Its surface is very uneven. It has both smooth and hilly areas. There's also what looks like a small mountain that rises 396 m (1,300 ft.) from its centre. The comet rotates once on its **axis** about every two Earth days.

Coma

Nucleus

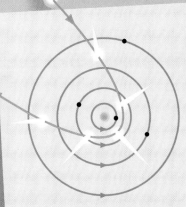

Why Does a Comet's Tail Always Point Away from the Sun?

The Sun is the reason a comet's tail points the way it does. Remember, a comet often has two tails—an ion tail and a dust tail. The ion tail is like a giant windsock. Pushed by the solar wind, it always streams away from the Sun. Meanwhile, the comet's dust tail is also forced behind the comet, but by intense pressure from particles of sunlight. Even after the comet has swung around the Sun and started its return trip to the outer reaches of the solar system, it continues to point away from the Sun. It goes tail first!

Meteorites Meteors, and Meteoroids

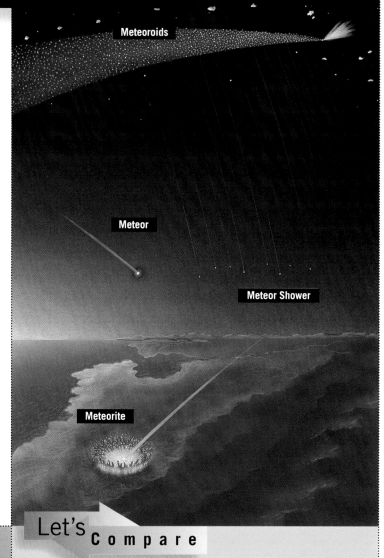

Meteoroids

Meteor

Meteor Shower

Meteorite

On April 26, 1803, the town of Laigle, France, was suddenly bombarded by more than 3,000 tiny space rocks. After the unusual shower had ended, the startled residents collected many of the rocks, which are called **meteorites.**

Every day millions of bits of cosmic debris hurtle through Earth's **atmosphere.** Some of these objects are the dusty remains of **comets** and others are chips off **asteroids.** They range in size from microscopic **dust** particles to rocks several kilograms in weight.

Over a period of a year about 400,000 tons of material rain down on Earth. Luckily, only a tenth of this actually reaches the ground; most burns up in the atmosphere. The objects are called **meteoroids** until they land on the ground. If they burn up in a streak of light before reaching the ground, they have yet another name: **meteors.**

Rarely does anybody see a meteorite hit the ground. On the evening of October 9, 1992, however, Michelle Knapp of Peekskill, New York, USA, *heard* a meteorite crash. The football-sized space rock crushed the boot of her car as it sat in her driveway!

How **Big?**

Largest Meteorite

The world's largest known meteorite—named Hoba—was discovered in 1920 on a farm in Namibia, a country in southwest Africa. This 65-ton boulder fell to Earth in prehistoric times and has never been moved from the spot where it landed. It is about 3 m (9 ft.) long and 2.5 m (8 ft.) wide. If it had been any bigger, it probably would have broken apart as it plummeted through Earth's atmosphere.

Let's Compare

The Name Says It All

Most meteoroids—fragments from asteroids and dust from comets—remain in outer space. Some, however, become 'caught' by Earth's **gravity.** As they fall at tremendous speeds through Earth's atmosphere, they become white-hot and begin to burn up, leaving a glowing trail across the sky. These fleeting streaks of light are called meteors, or 'shooting stars'. Occasionally, several dozen or more meteors fall in an hour—an event known as a meteor shower.

Most meteors last only a few seconds. Larger pieces, however, sometimes survive their free fall to Earth. The fragments that reach the ground are called meteorites.

Meteor Showers and Storms

On any dark, clear night, about 10 meteors can be seen streaking across the sky each hour. But at certain times of the year *(right)*, when Earth crosses the dusty path of a comet, meteors become so common that they appear to 'shower' from the sky. A well-known meteor shower happens every August, when Earth crosses the path of the Swift-Tuttle comet. At this time, up to 50 meteors or more can be spotted each hour. On very rare occasions, a shower will turn into a meteor storm of thousands of meteors an hour.

Meteors fill the night sky during the spectacular meteor storm of November 13, 1833 *(left)*.

Date of Maximum Activity	Meteor Shower Name	Rough Hourly Count	Parent Comet
Jan. 3	Quadrantid	40	Unknown
April 22	Lyrid	10	Thatcher
May 4	Eta Aquarid	20	Halley
July 29	Delta Aquarid	20	Unknown
Aug. 12	Perseid	50	Swift-Tuttle
Oct. 9	Draconid	500	Giacobini-Zinner
Oct. 21	Orionid	30	Halley
Nov. 3	Southern Taurid	10	Encke
Nov. 16	Leonid	12*	Tempel-Tuttle
Dec. 13	Geminid	50	3200 Phaethon

*Every 33 years, this can jump up to 1,000 meteors per minute.

Fireballs

A very bright meteor is called a fireball. On August 10, 1972, a huge fireball streaked through Earth's upper atmosphere. It is shown here above the Grand Teton Mountains in the western United States. The meteoroid that caused the fireball probably weighed as much as 1,000 tons. Fortunately, it skipped off the atmosphere like a stone skipping off the surface of water, and headed back into space.

Giant Impacts

Every 10,000 years or so a really big **meteorite**—bigger than a small house—slams into Earth. These gigantic space 'bombs' create spectacular flashes of light as they rocket through the **atmosphere** at speeds of up to 15 km (9 miles) per second. When they hit Earth, they explode with tremendous force.

Fortunately most of these larger meteorites—like the one that created Barringer Meteor Crater in Arizona, USA, *(opposite page)*—cause only local damage. However, sometimes Earth collides with a **meteoroid** so huge that it leads to a global catastrophe—like the one that is believed to have killed off the dinosaurs 65 million years ago.

There are more than 2,000 large **asteroids** and **comets** whose **orbits** cross that of Earth. Any one of them could one day make a direct hit on the **planet.** Scientists are now trying to devise better systems of tracking these threatening near-Earth objects. They also hope to develop some way of deflecting or destroying them before the next one smashes into Earth.

How Small? Microcraters

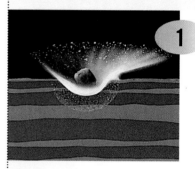

Tiny **craters**—even microscopic ones—look just like big ones. The photograph at left is of a tiny grain of glassy material from the **Moon.** It has been magnified 100 times. The crater, called a microcrater, was formed when the grain was hit by an even smaller particle of cosmic **dust.**

Creating a Crater

Meteorite craters are not just 'holes in the ground'. Their saucer-like shape is the result of a powerful explosion. The steps below explain how they get this unique shape.

1 When a meteorite slams into a planet or moon, it sends shock waves *(white arc)* down into the ground. These forceful waves pulverize the surface. Dust and broken bits of rock are thrown up and out like splashing water.

The meteorite quickly breaks apart and explodes. Heat from the explosion melts some of the meteorite as well as rock below it. The red-hot liquid rock lines the crater, which grows wider.

2

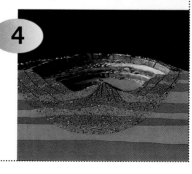

3 When the shock waves end, the crater stops growing. The rock and dust fall back to the ground, forming a raised edge around the crater. Sometimes the floor of the crater rises up, creating a rocky peak in the centre.

As the peak on the crater floor rises it tugs on the walls. This causes the walls to slide down and inward, giving them a step-like appearance.

4

A Smash Hit

Scientists believe that huge meteorites were the cause of about 100 gigantic craters around the world. One is Barringer Meteor Crater in the USA *(below)*. About 50,000 years ago a 300,000-ton meteorite hit the ground and created this crater, which is 168 m (550 ft.) deep and more than 1,200 m (4,000 ft.) wide. The largest craters can only be seen in full from space. A 200-million-year-old crater in Canada is now the Manicouagan Reservoir *(right)*. It is 66 km (41 miles) wide. The reservoir, here covered in ice, surrounds a huge island—the crater's central peak.

Where Did All the Dinos Go?

Dinosaurs suddenly disappeared from Earth about 65 million years ago. What happened to them? Many scientists now think dinosaurs were killed off by a comet or asteroid colliding with Earth. When the enormous object hit, it exploded with such force that huge amounts of dust were blasted into the **atmosphere.** For many months sunlight could not get through, and the planet turned dark and cold. Under such harsh conditions, about 80 percent of Earth's plants and animals died.

Tunguska Flattened!

On the morning of June 30, 1908, people living in a remote area of Russia called Tunguska saw a large, bluish white streak race across the sky. Moments later, they heard a tremendous explosion—one so powerful it knocked people off their feet 60 km (37 miles) away. No one was near enough to the explosion to be killed, but the force of the explosion instantly flattened trees for up to 18 km (11 miles). Scientists now believe an asteroid or comet entered Earth's atmosphere and exploded in midair. No crater or other evidence of an impacting body has ever been found.

What Is Astronomy?

Astronomy is the study of **stars, planets, comets,** and other celestial bodies—that is, objects in space. It is the study of regions of space and of the universe as a whole. It is one of the oldest sciences.

People were gazing at the stars long before clocks and calendars, compasses, and tide charts were invented. Before these tools became available, tracking the regular movements of the stars and other objects in the sky was the only way ancient people could tell what time of day or year it was, which direction to go when they were travelling, and when they might expect a high or low tide.

Today, sophisticated instruments combined with computers put such information at your fingertips. But if you were marooned on a desert island, a crash course in **astronomy** would be a very handy thing! Modern astronomers continue to map space and the movement of objects. They measure the universe and debate its origins. Though their science has become much more complex than that of the earliest stargazers, modern astronomers still build on the work of the ancients.

What's in a Name?

Astronomy

The word 'astronomy' comes from the Greek words 'astron', which means 'star', and 'nemein', meaning 'to name'. The first astronomers were probably shepherds who watched the sky for changes in the positions of stars and other celestial objects so they could predict changes in the seasons.

Early Calendar

Most early civilizations measured the passing of time by the phases of the Moon. To the Egyptians, one month was one lunar cycle—the 29 or 30 days from one new moon to the next. Their first calendars (right) split the year into three four-month seasons (circles). The year began when the Dog Star Sirius (the goddess Isis to them) rose in the east just before dawn. The arrival of Sirius also told them that the Nile River would flood and it was time to plant their crops.

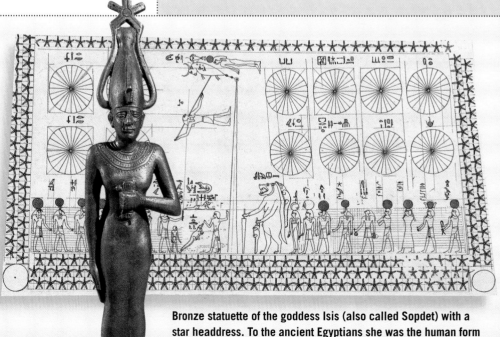

Bronze statuette of the goddess Isis (also called Sopdet) with a star headdress. To the ancient Egyptians she was the human form of the star Sirius.

Early Record Keepers

Teachers like to tell their pupils, 'Take good notes!' Well, your teacher would approve of the Babylonians, an ancient people that flourished from 2700 BC to 538 BC. They lived in the part of the world that is now the country of Iraq. The Babylonians kept careful astronomical records on clay tablets *(right)*. A translation of the wedge-shaped writing (called cuneiform) reveals remarkably accurate observations about the movements of Venus and other planets, the phases of the Moon, **eclipses,** and so on. These detailed records helped the Babylonians predict when the new moon would appear so they could schedule feast days

and plan the planting and harvesting of crops. Hundreds of years later, the Greek astronomer Hipparchus used the clay Babylonian records to help him calculate Earth's precession (how much it wobbles on its axis).

Hipparchus, who lived in about 150 BC, was considered the greatest Greek astronomer. By carefully studying the night sky, he brought the number of named stars to more than 850. This painting shows him using a simple tube to look at stars: the telescope wasn't invented until 1608.

People Benjamin Banneker

Benjamin Banneker was the first African American astronomer and scientist. He became interested in astronomy in 1771, when he was 40 years old. A friend lent him two astronomy books, a telescope, and some drawing instruments. Soon he was predicting the positions of stars and planets in the sky. He even successfully predicted a **solar eclipse,** a very difficult feat at the time. In 1792, he started publishing his predictions in a best-selling almanac. It was a valuable resource for many people. Sailors used its information for navigation, and farmers used it to figure out the best time to plant crops.

What's an Astronomer?

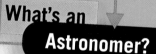

An astronomer studies objects in the universe, what they're made of, and how they move. Astronomer Sandra Faber focuses on **galaxies**—how they formed, their shapes, and how fast they are moving through space. Powerful telescopes give her a window deep into the universe.

Pictures sent back by the Hubble Space Telescope *(page 106)* give her a close look at the centres of distant galaxies, where she looks for black holes. However, being an astronomer can be hazardous. Early in her career, she fell off a telescope platform and knocked herself out!

Ancient Observatories

I magine what it would be like if there were no clocks or calendars. How would you know what time it was, or whether it was March or July? Being sure of the season would be especially difficult in parts of the world where temperatures don't change much throughout the year.

This was a challenge faced by early civilizations. But they soon discovered that objects in the sky seemed to move in regular patterns and that they could use these movements to help them chart the passing of time. For example, the path the Sun takes across the sky and how high it goes changes slightly depending on the time of year. Early people built structures on Earth that were precisely aligned to the motions of the Sun, the Moon, and the **stars.** You have only to look at these first observatories to marvel at the highly sophisticated astronomical calculations that were possible with such simple structures.

Wheel of the Sun

T he Bighorn Medicine Wheel *(below)* was a huge stone calendar built by early Native Americans living in the Bighorn Mountains of Wyoming, USA. Piles of rocks, called 'cairns', were lined up with the annual movements of the Sun and three other stars—Aldebaran, Sirius, and Rigel. The Sun rises over different cairns during the summer and winter solstices— the times of year when it is highest and lowest in the sky, signalling the arrival of summer and winter.

The Mystery of the Stones

Stonehenge, England's most famous ruins, is also one of its greatest mysteries. No one knows for sure why these huge stones were placed in a circle some 4,000 years ago, but many people think they were used by Stone Age astronomers to keep track of the seasons. You see, where the Sun rises and sets changes slightly throughout the year. If you stand at the centre of the stones you can see the Sun rise over different stones at different times of year. In this picture, the Sun's position relative to one of the stones announces the beginning of summer on the day of the summer solstice.

Stargazing Tools of Long Ago

KOREA

Early observations of celestial objects were made with the naked eye from simple stone structures that dotted the landscape of the ancient world. The world's oldest observatory that's still standing is the Chomsung-dae Observatory in Kyongju, South Korea. Built in AD 632, it's not much more than a stone tower with an open roof.

MEXICO

The Caracol, built at Chichén Itzá about AD 1000, is believed to have been a Mayan observatory. A spiral staircase inside leads up to a series of windows that are carefully aligned with the rising and setting of the Sun and other stars at different times of the year.

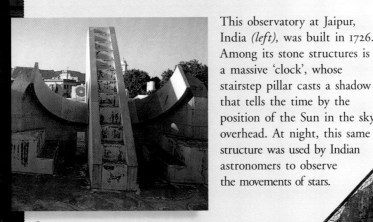

INDIA

This observatory at Jaipur, India *(left)*, was built in 1726. Among its stone structures is a massive 'clock', whose stairstep pillar casts a shadow that tells the time by the position of the Sun in the sky overhead. At night, this same structure was used by Indian astronomers to observe the movements of stars.

Daggers and Serpents

Not all ancient observatories were monumental in size. In 1977 an artist climbing Chaco Canyon, in New Mexico, USA, stumbled across a spiral rock carving partly hidden behind tall boulders. It was the work of the long-gone Anasazi Indians. At midday on the summer solstice, a dramatic dagger of sunlight slashes across the spiral.

No less dramatic is the serpent created by shadows on the stairway of a Mayan pyramid on Mexico's Yucatán Peninsula. At the base of the stairs is a serpent's head carved from stone. Briefly twice a year the serpent gets a sunlit body. Builders of the pyramid positioned it so that at sunset on the equinox—the two days of the year when day and night are equal in length—sunlight and shadows are cast so as to create the undulating body.

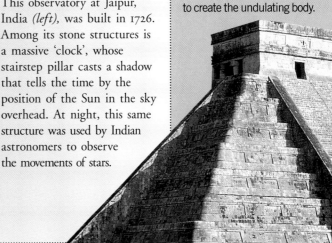

Two Views _{of the} ^{Universe}

Earth in the Middle

S tand outside at night and watch the **stars** move across the sky. Earth appears to stand still, with everything else in space moving around it. So it seemed to the first astronomers.

For thousands of years, astronomers held a geocentric view of the universe. They thought everything in the universe moved around the Earth. This system of planetary motion is called the Ptolemaic system, named for Greek astronomer Ptolemy, who lived in about AD 150.

One thousand four hundred years after Ptolemy, Polish astronomer Nicolaus Copernicus turned **astronomy** on its head. He revived a theory first proposed by an ancient Greek astronomer named Aristarchus (310-230 BC). He presented the shocking idea that all of the planets, including Earth, revolve around the Sun. This is known as the heliocentric, or Sun-centred, view of the universe—widely known as the Copernican system.

Copernicus's theory was correct, of course, but most people did not believe it back then. His work was opposed not only by other scientists but also by the Roman Catholic Church, which considered his system dangerous to its teachings. The Copernican system wouldn't be widely accepted for another 100 years.

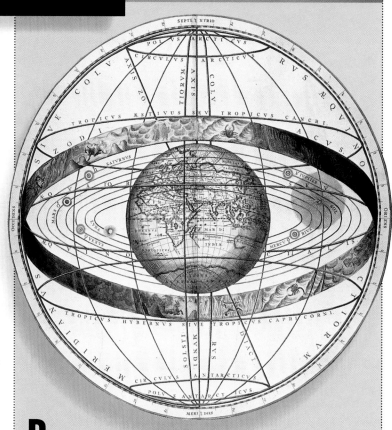

P tolemy's model of the universe *(above)* had the Sun, Moon, and planets travelling in perfect circles around the Earth. All of these celestial objects fitted inside a huge sphere of stars. He also thought the planets revolved in little circles—called epicycles —as they moved about the Earth. Ptolemy's view of the universe survived for 1,500 years.

The Sun Takes Centre Stage

Copernicus *(right)* put the Sun— not Earth—at the centre of the universe. This drawing of the Copernican system from a 17th-century celestial atlas *(left)* shows that Earth with its Moon was just one of the six known **planets** of the time to circle the Sun. Copernicus even placed the planets in the proper order—Mercury and Venus between Earth and the Sun, and Mars, Jupiter, and Saturn between Earth and the stars.

Tycho Brahe

Danish astronomer Tycho Brahe was the greatest of the pre-telescopic star observers. The king of Denmark built him an observatory *(below),* and from there Tycho collected 20 years of detailed records. These records were used by later astronomers to prove Copernicus's heliocentric model of the universe. Tycho came up with his own model of the universe that fell somewhere between the Copernican and the Ptolemaic views. He believed that Earth was at the centre and that the Sun and the Moon revolved around it. But all the other planets, he thought, went around the Sun. (An unrelated, but interesting, fact about Tycho is that his nose was sliced off in a duel. For the rest of his life, he wore a metal nose cap.)

Kepler

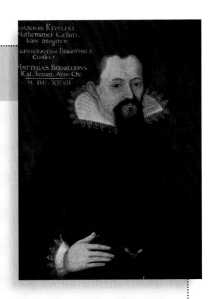

Tycho Brahe's last assistant was German mathematician Johannes Kepler, with whom Tycho left all his astronomical records. Unlike Tycho, Kepler leaned toward Copernicus's view of the universe. Now, using Tycho's careful measurements, Kepler formulated three laws of planetary motion. The first law states that all the planets **orbit** the Sun in **elliptical** paths. The second law shows, in part, that a planet's speed around the Sun is not constant, but changes with distance from the Sun. The third law links the time it takes for a planet to complete an orbit and its distance from the Sun. With this work, Kepler discredited the Ptolemaic system. However, before he came up with these brilliant laws, he had some pretty kooky ideas. He believed, for instance, that the orbital speeds of the planets could be reproduced musically *(below).*

Galileo Gets a Good Look

In 1609 Italian astronomer Galileo Galilei became the first person to turn a telescope *(left)* toward the heavens and record what he saw. He changed the face of science forever. For the first time, scientists could see things that were not visible to the naked eye alone. Using his telescope, Galileo disproved, once and for all, the Ptolemaic system. In doing so, he made a powerful enemy: the Roman Catholic Church. In 1633, the Church forced Galileo to renounce his work and live out his life under house arrest. The Church didn't get around to admitting he was right until 1992!

Optical Telescopes

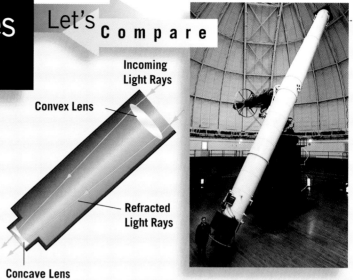

When Italian astronomer Galileo tipped his homemade telescope up to the heavens in 1609, it was the first time any scientist had used a tool that could extend one's vision of the universe. Today the telescope is still the principal tool of **astronomy,** bringing celestial objects and events closer to yield their secrets. Telescopes that give us a closer look at objects that are visible to human eyes are called optical telescopes. There are two types. The **refracting telescope** was perfected and used by Galileo himself. Later, Isaac Newton added a new breed of optical telescope: the **reflecting telescope.** Despite changes in size and style, optical telescopes are still based on the same principles Galileo and Newton knew: fixed lenses that bend—or refract—light, and fixed mirrors that reflect light.

Refracting Telescope

When light travels through curved glass, it bends, or refracts. A convex, or bulging, curve refracts light inward. A concave, or cupped, curve refracts light outward. In a refracting telescope, light rays from the object viewed collect on the convex lens and are focused inward. A smaller, concave lens magnifies the image. The world's largest refracting telescope—the one at Yerkes Observatory, in Wisconsin, USA *(above)*—has a large lens that is 100 cm (40 in.) across.

Would You Believe?

Child's Play: A Telescope

Inventing the telescope may have been child's play to Dutch spectacle maker Hans Lippershey—literally. In 1608, according to one account, two children were playing with some lenses in Lippershey's workshop. When they looked through two of them at a church nearby, the church appeared much larger! Lippershey at once tried it out for himself and was amazed. To make it easier to look through the lenses, he mounted them in a tube—the first telescope!

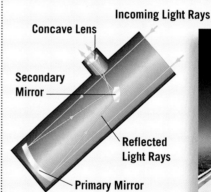

Reflecting Telescope

Though early astronomers saw marvellous things through the refracting telescope, these first telescopes were not very good. Isaac Newton experimented with mirrors to devise a better one, and the reflecting telescope was born. This type of telescope catches light on a large, concave, primary mirror, which reflects the light up to a smaller, secondary mirror. From here the image is magnified by a concave lens. In large research telescopes, the image is sent to a camera or other instrument attached to the telescope. Shown above is the New Technology Telescope, a large reflector at the European Southern Observatory on Cerro La Silla, Chile.

How High?

Observatories provide the best views of space when they are located in remote places away from city lights. It also helps if they are high enough so there is not a lot of air turbulence. Earth's largest optical telescopes, Keck I and Keck II, are sited 4,205 m (13,790 ft.) above sea level on Hawaii's Mauna Kea *(left),* an extinct—astronomers hope!—volcano.

Underground Sun

You could really damage your eyes if you looked at the Sun through a telescope, so you need a special kind. The McMath-Pierce Solar Telescope, on Kitt Peak, Arizona, USA, is a telescope designed just for studying the Sun. In it a 200-cm (80-in.) rotating mirror, or heliostat, guides sunlight down a 150-m (492-ft.) tunnel—buried to keep temperatures constant. At the tunnel's end, a 150-cm (60-in.) mirror collects the light and reflects it to a smaller, secondary mirror, which flashes it down to the observation room below. Scientists can look at an image of the Sun *(far left)* or they can direct the light to any of a number of instruments, including **spectrographs,** which separate the Sun's light into a rainbow **spectrum** *(page 21)* that tells them what the Sun is made of.

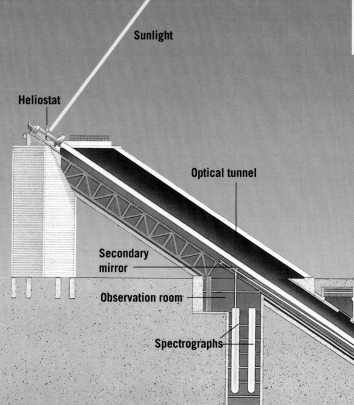

Sunlight

Heliostat

Optical tunnel

Secondary mirror

Observation room

Spectrographs

Primary mirror

A solar telescope enables scientists to see the Sun's fiery surface, or photosphere, dotted with cooler sunspots.

Radio Telescopes

Arecibo

Optical telescopes capture **visible-light** radiation. But there is more to **radiation** than meets the eye. Radio waves, for example, are invisible cousins of light rays *(see* **electromagnetic spectrum,** *pages* 16-17*).* They are made of the same stuff, but radio waves have longer **wavelengths** that our eyes can't see.

Many objects in space give off radio waves, but we didn't know that until 1932. An American scientist named Karl Jansky made the discovery when he was trying to find the source of bothersome static interfering with radio communication. Using homemade equipment, Jansky tracked the interfering radio waves to their source. To his astonishment, they were coming from a constellation near the centre of the Milky Way!

Since then, scientists have used radio telescopes to 'see' things in space that they couldn't see before. They can't actually see the radio waves, but they can see pictures of them produced by radio telescopes *(opposite).*

In a natural limestone valley in the rain forest of Puerto Rico lies the world's biggest single-dish radio telescope, the Arecibo reflector, named for a nearby town. A patchwork metal dish that's 305 m (1,000 ft.) across creates a 7-hectare (18-acre) collecting surface. The dish itself doesn't move, but the structure suspended above it moves so it can collect all the radio waves reflected by the dish. Arecibo is more than just the biggest single-dish radio telescope; it also ranks as the most sensitive telescope of its kind. It has been used to study **pulsars,** and map molecular and atomic **gas** in the universe. It has even been used to listen for broadcasts from extraterrestrial civilizations that may exist elsewhere in the universe.

Beneath Arecibo's giant dish is a lush landscape of tropical plants that thrive in the moist, shaded space. The dish is made up of almost 40,000 adjustable aluminium panels.

Spanning a Continent

Imagine a radio telescope that stretches from Hawaii, across North America, to an island in the Caribbean—a telescope 8,000 km (5,000 miles) long. In fact, such a marvel exists, and here's how it works: a radio telescope dish doesn't need to be continuous. You can string 10 different dishes across the hemisphere and have them all work as one gargantuan telescope. The VLBA—Very Long Baseline Array—operated by the U.S. National Radio Astronomy Observatory, has been scoping out the stars since 1993.

How a Radio Telescope Works

Though radio telescopes look very different from optical telescopes, and are made of different materials, mechanically they have similarities. Radio telescopes must be much bigger, however, because radio waves are so much bigger than visible-light waves. The large dish collects radio waves from space and bounces them back up to a feed antenna poised above the dish. The antenna sends the signal to an amplifier, which turns the radio waves into an electrical signal. A computer then changes this signal into an image *(below)*.

Radio Pictures

Would **You** *Believe?*

Radio waves can't carry music or pictures, but they can be turned into them by special instruments. You hear words and music coming out of your radio because a transmitter at the radio station has manipulated the radio waves so they carry these audible sounds. In a similar way, radio telescopes change radio waves coming from space into pictures *(right)*. Using radio telescopes, astronomers have discovered objects in space they never knew existed and they have seen familiar sights, such as Jupiter *(near right)*, in a completely new way. They have peered deep into the centre of the Milky Way **galaxy** *(far right, top)* and seen the gaseous remains of giant **stars** that exploded aeons ago, such as Cassiopeia A *(far right, bottom)*.

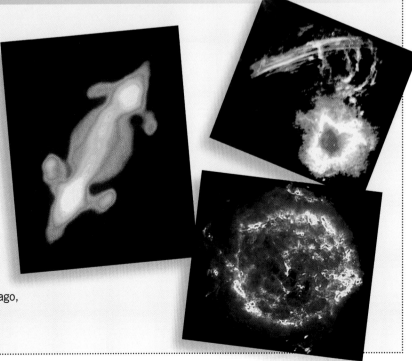

Hubble Space Telescope

Though astronomers have made amazing observations through their Earth-bound telescopes over the last 400 years, planet Earth makes a lousy stargazing platform. Air turbulence causes blurry viewing. Light pollution—the illumination of the night sky by light from cities, towns, and other human sources—creates a hazy glow. And Earth's **atmosphere** itself scatters and absorbs some of the light from stars, so less of the light gets to a telescope. What astronomers really need is an eye in the sky—and as of 1990 they have one. Launched into orbit from the cargo bay of the space shuttle 600 km (380 miles) up, the Hubble Space Telescope circles the **planet** every 96 minutes. Whizzing along at 29,000 km/h (18,000 mph), it beams back a steady stream of awe-inspiring images of the **cosmos,** from tiny **asteroids** in our **solar system** to **galaxy** clusters a billion times bigger at the far edge of the universe.

Let's Compare

Hubble's Sharp Eyes

Ask an astronomer what's so great about Hubble, and he or she might launch into a talk about resolution in arc seconds that'll make your head spin. Here's the bottom line: at any given moment, Hubble can see 10 times better than the best telescope on Earth. The small image above of galaxy M33 was taken from the Earth-bound Hale Telescope. See the tiny outlined box? That spot—called NGC 604—is shown greatly enlarged in a snapshot by Hubble, at top. Isn't that amazing!

Hubble is a **reflecting telescope,** collecting images on a primary mirror that is 2.4 m (94 in.) across. It carries cameras for visible and infrared light, a **spectrograph,** and instruments to measure the positions of **stars.** Hubble uses its two communication antennas to send the images it gets as radio signals to **satellites** orbiting the Earth. These then beam the information to antennas on Earth's surface. Through these same satellites, Earth-bound astronomers can direct Hubble's 'eyes' to regions of the universe. Solar panels collect energy to power the instruments.

The Space Telescope Close Up

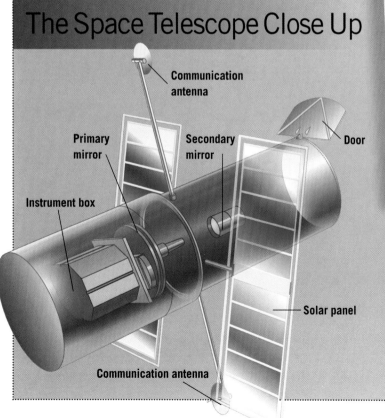

- Communication antenna
- Primary mirror
- Secondary mirror
- Door
- Instrument box
- Solar panel
- Communication antenna

Space-Eye Surgery

Launched with fanfare in 1990, Hubble could see 10 times better than telescopes on Earth. Or could it? To the growing dismay of astronomers, it became clear that Hubble was nearsighted. The problem? Its primary mirror was off by one-fiftieth the width of a human hair—enough to ruin its eyesight! In 1993, as an admiring world watched, space shuttle astronauts snagged the orbiting telescope and spent 35 hours making repairs *(left)*. Here it is seen orbiting over western Australia. Its vision restored, Hubble has gone on to fulfil all of its original promise.

Would You Believe?

A Runaway Planet!

Scientists would like to believe they are seeing a runaway planet in this Hubble photo, but they aren't sure. If it is a planet, it's three times more massive than our biggest planet, Jupiter. And it would be the first picture ever taken of a planet outside our **solar system.** The suspected planet, seen at the bottom of the photo, is connected to a double star by a long trail of light. Scientists believe that the gravitational forces of the double star gave it the boot and sent it hurtling into space, leaving this glowing trail in its wake.

Robot Observers

Planetary Visits

Space probes are the robotic scouts of the space age. These versatile pioneers went to the Moon before humans did and have flown deep into the **solar system,** far beyond where any human has ventured. They have sent us back tantalizing glimpses of Jupiter's **moons,** Saturn's rings, Halley's **comet,** and the barren surfaces of Mars and Venus—close-in views no telescope can match. Take *Voyager* I, for example. Launched way back in 1977, it is now hurtling toward 'termination shock', the mysterious edge of the solar system where the Sun's influence ends and interstellar space takes over. Then there's *Sojourner,* the plucky robotic rover that rolled around the surface of Mars as people watched, rivetted to their television sets. *Voyager* and *Sojourner* are just two of the many space-age robots taking scientists, and us, to places humans may not get to for another century—or 10.

How Far?

Voyager's Travels

As of 1998, unmanned space probe *Voyager 1* was 10.5 billion km (6.5 billion miles) away—almost twice as far as Pluto is from us! And it has enough electricity to keep it going until about 2020. By then, it will be 22 billion km (14 billion miles) out, in the dark, icy realm of interstellar space. Will it run into intelligent life forms? If so, it is prepared to give them a taste of life on Earth. On board this tiny ambassador from Earth is a time capsule containing music, greetings, and many photos, including this one of children.

In 1962 *Mariner 2* became the first successful space probe to visit another **planet.** It flew by Venus and sent back data about the hot, cloud-covered world. Since then, many more probes have followed, journeying to seven of the eight other planets. Only Pluto has not been visited. The list below shows the first probe to each planet and other important probes, as well as their arrival dates.

Mariner 10 (1974, 1975) — **Mercury**

Mariner 2 (1962)
Venera 4, 7, 9, 13, 14 (1967, 1970, 1975, 1982)
Mariner 10 (1974)
Pioneer Venus 1, 2 (1978)
Magellan (1990) — **Venus**

Mariner 4, 9 (1965, 1971)
Viking 1, 2 (1976)
Mars Pathfinder (1997)
Mars Global Surveyor (1997) — **Mars**

Pioneer 10, 11 (1973, 1974)
Voyager 1, 2 (1979)
Galileo (1995) — **Jupiter**

Pioneer 11 (1979)
Voyager 1, 2 (1980, 1981)
Cassini (expected arrival 2004) — **Saturn**

Voyager 2 (1986) — **Uranus**

Voyager 2 (1989) — **Neptune**

Mission to Mars

It took *Global Surveyor* 10 months to reach Mars. Once it got there, the probe had an ambitious mission: to map the planet and make high-quality observations of its magnetic and gravitational fields. Launched in 1997, the probe was slowed down by structural damage. But this didn't stop the rugged little scout from beaming back fascinating glimpses of the Red Planet's hilly surface *(right)*.

The Little Probe That Could

When Halley's comet made its latest swing by Earth in 1986, five space probes raced out to meet it. Four **satellites** already in space turned their eyes in its direction. Scientists had never before been able to get a close look at a comet, and this was their chance. One of the probes, *Giotto (right)*, flew so close that it was almost knocked out by the comet! But it survived and sent back amazing pictures of the comet's tiny **nucleus**—the dirty chunk of ice that forms the heart of a comet *(page 91)*.

Painting by Numbers

The Royal Mail doesn't deliver from space. So how do those fascinating pictures make it home? It's painting by numbers. Here's how a picture of a Martian **crater** was sent to us on Earth. Light sensors on a spacecraft broke down the crater into 'pixels' *(centre)*— short for 'picture elements'. An on-board computer then assigned each pixel a number based on how bright it was *(bottom)*. The numbers were transmitted to Earth, where a computer translated them back into the kind of picture human eyes can read *(top)*. It's no surprise that optical engineers at NASA are nicknamed 'pixel pushers'.

Would You Believe?

We're always told not to litter, but in space that's not easy to do. As yet, no one has figured out a good way to bring jettisoned gear back to Earth. Take the Moon, for example. Numerous space probes have crash-landed on its surface, and human visitors have left behind tons of stuff. Because the Moon has no **atmosphere**, things don't rot. What's left there, stays there. Here's a list of some of the lunar litter dropped by human beings.

Lunar Litter

More than 20 space probes

3 moon buggies

6 American flags

6 jettisoned lunar landers

1 two-wheeled lunar cart

2 Soviet medals

1 gold olive branch

1 disk with goodwill messages

1 photo of astronaut's family

2 golf balls

Human Space Exploration

Dreams of Flight

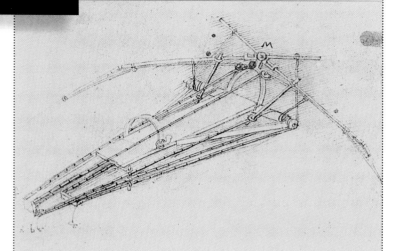

What young dreamer hasn't turned to the night sky and imagined travelling to those distant flickering **stars?** It is human destiny, wrote Russian rocket scientist Konstantin Tsiolkovsky (1857-1935), 'to set foot on the soil of the **asteroids,** to lift by hand a rock from the Moon. . . .'. Tsiolkovsky did more than dream. His innovative ideas included the notion that rockets could be built in stages, so that fuel tanks could drop away as they emptied—a necessity for modern spaceflight.

Though dreams of the stars inspired scientists to tinker with rocketry, war and politics pushed the science forward. During World War II, both sides raced to develop rockets that could deliver weapons. Afterwards, the United States and the U.S.S.R. became locked in what was called the 'space race', each striving for the highest ground: space. In 1957, the Soviets were the first to get an object into space, when they launched the artificial **satellite** *Sputnik 1*—its name means 'fellow traveller' in Russian. The intense competition speeded up the pace of progress. Just 12 years later, two American astronauts walked—or, more accurately, bounced!—on the Moon. The age of human space exploration had begun.

Humans have long dreamed of flying through the air and travelling to the stars. Leonardo da Vinci (1452-1519), the famous Italian Renaissance painter and inventor, was one such dreamer. He studied the flight of birds and laboured for 25 years to develop a machine that flew like them. Two of his designs are shown here. To fly the machine above, a person would lie down in it and operate wings at shoulder height, flapping them up and down. Not even a genius like Leonardo could make this work. Modern engineers are more impressed by the invention shown below, from another of Leonardo's notebooks. The huge screw-like propeller, called a helical screw, works on the same principle as a modern-day helicopter. Today's readers of Leonardo's notebooks are perhaps equally amazed by the fact that he wrote them all backwards! Words run from right to left across the page, and letters are reversed, as you can see in a portion of one of his notebook pages below.

Fast FACTS

1957 Laika the dog becomes the first living creature in space

1961 Yuri Gagarin is the first human to orbit the Earth

1961 Alan Shepard is the first American in space

1962 John Glenn is the first American to orbit the Earth

1963 Valentina Tereshkova is the first woman in space

1965 Alexei Leonov takes the first spacewalk

1968 *Apollo 8* carries the first humans around the Moon

1969 Neil Armstrong becomes the first human on the Moon

1971 *Salyut 1* is the first space station to orbit the Earth

1973 *Skylab* is the first American space station

1981 *Columbia* is launched as the first space shuttle

1983 Sally Ride is the first American woman in space

Kicking Off the Space Age

Small but no lightweight, the first satellite, *Sputnik* 1, measured a scant 59 cm (23 in.) across but weighed a heavy 83 kg (184 lb.). It had a big impact for such a little thing, too, triggering a space race between the United States and its rival the Soviet Union that eventually led to humans in space and the numerous space-age technologies used on Earth today. Where is *Sputnik* now? It splashed into the ocean and sank, three months after making history.

Animal Astronauts

Before the first human flew into space, a number of animal astronauts went up to make sure it would be safe. One was a chimp named Ham. The furry astronaut trained for more than a year before taking his flight, which propelled him 253 km (157 miles) above the Earth in 1961. Strapped into a special seat *(above)*, he endured a little more than six minutes of weightlessness before falling back down to Earth. Happily, he was safely scooped out of the ocean.

First Man in Space

Yuri Gagarin, a Soviet cosmonaut, was the first man—and the first human—ever to go into space. He orbited Earth for 108 minutes in *Vostok 1*, on April 12, 1961. Then his retrorocket fired, pointing him back toward Earth. When he reached a safe altitude in the **atmosphere** he ejected from the spacecraft and parachuted down to the surface.

First Woman in Space

Two years after the first man orbited in space, the Soviets sent up a female cosmonaut. Valentina Tereshkova spent three days in space before reentering Earth's atmosphere and parachuting to the surface. The relaxed cosmonaut gave ground controllers a few anxious moments by sleeping through a radio transmission!

First Step on the Moon

NASA planned the first Moon landing for the Fourth of July. But minor technical glitches slowed things down, and it wasn't until July 20, 1969, that Neil Armstrong and Buzz Aldrin became the first humans to walk on the lunar surface. People glued to their televisions watched intently as Armstrong took the first historic step and said these words: 'That's one small step for [a] man, one giant leap for mankind'.

Living in Space

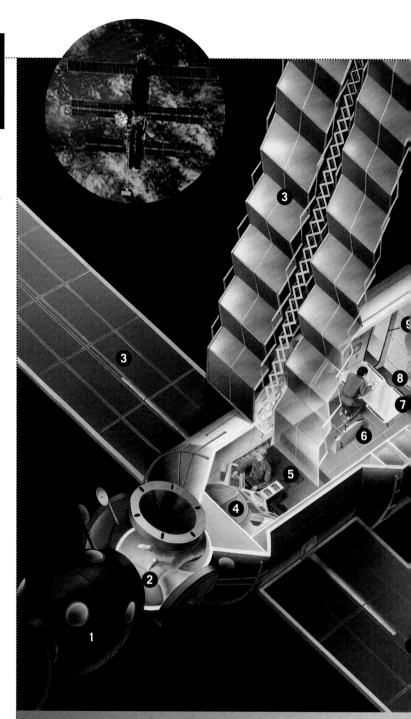

Since 1971, scores of Russian cosmonauts and American astronauts have pioneered life in space. They have put up with cramped quarters, food squeezed out of tubes, little privacy, loneliness, and what seems like endless bossy orders from Earth. The hope is that their experiences will make it possible for humans to visit other worlds one day.

Their hardship hasn't been in vain. One by one, problems are being overcome. The stations are quieter, so crews sleep better. Food is tastier, helping cosmonauts overcome a dangerous loss of appetite. Elf-sized cabins provide privacy. Schedules allow time for just hanging out. And strenuous exercise routines combat the muscle wasting and bone thinning that occur in zero gravity.

On the technical side, engineers are improving on-board recycling of oxygen and water, so that space stations—and future space travellers—can be more self-sufficient.

I Was There!

In 1996, astronaut Shannon Lucid was on board the Russian space station *Mir* when she set an American duration record for time in space. What was it like spending 188 days in a tin can in space? Laughed Lucid, 'It's like living in a camper in the back of your pickup with your kids . . . when it's raining and no one can get out!' But the most important lesson she said she learned from the experience was that 'the crew has to be compatible and get along and work together'.

What Life Is Like on *Mir*

Launched in 1986, the Russian space station *Mir* can hold three resident cosmonauts and up to three visitors in very tight quarters. Cosmonauts work mostly in the forward control section and eat and exercise in the central part. Soundproof curtains seal off two private cabins—each no bigger than a small telephone booth—to help the crew sleep well. Outside, large solar panels generate electricity for the space station, and six docking ports allow other vessels to hook up. In the painting above, an escape vehicle is at one port and a research vessel is docked at another.

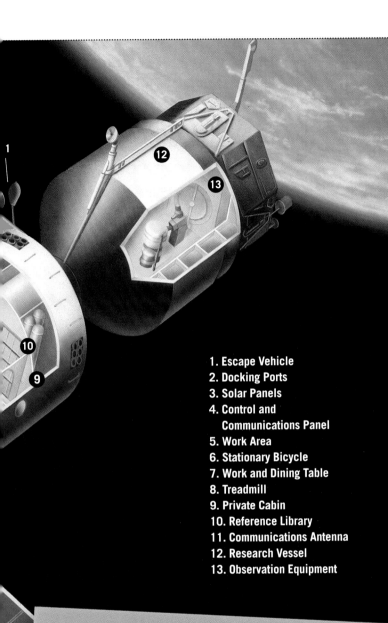

1. Escape Vehicle
2. Docking Ports
3. Solar Panels
4. Control and Communications Panel
5. Work Area
6. Stationary Bicycle
7. Work and Dining Table
8. Treadmill
9. Private Cabin
10. Reference Library
11. Communications Antenna
12. Research Vessel
13. Observation Equipment

Co-operation Space Station

Coming soon to an **orbit** near you—well, about 350 km (220 miles) over your head, actually — is the International Space Station, a joint project of the United States, Russia, the European Space Agency, Japan, and several other countries. Inside, seven astronauts will have living space that's equal to two jumbo jet passenger cabins. Outside, the station is the size of 14 tennis courts—so huge it must be taken up in pieces and assembled in space. It will take American astronauts and Russian cosmonauts at least 800 hours to put the behemoth together. Now that's co-operation!

Space, Sweet Space

When you swim out of bed in the morning, use a suction toilet, and chase down a floating blob of escaped orange juice, you know you're not at home on Earth anymore. Weightlessness, the effect of zero **gravity,** is the single biggest change astronauts have to get used to. It can be fun, and you can get used to it, but over the long haul, it's a pain in the neck, report those who have experienced it for long periods of time.

On board *Skylab,* Charles Conrad giggles in the complicated-looking arrangement that passes for a bath in space. On *Mir,* Shannon Lucid had to stick with sponge baths for six months.

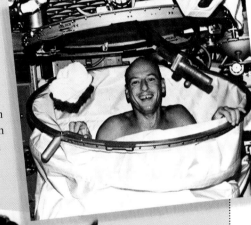

Sally Ride sleeps like a baby in a tethered sleeping bag aboard the space shuttle. Here's a plus: because soft tissue in your throat doesn't sag shut, there's no snoring in space!

To while away the hours in space, shuttle astronaut Loren Shriver perfects his sweet toss in zero gravity. He has plenty of time to catch the sweets, since they won't hit the floor until the craft returns to Earth!

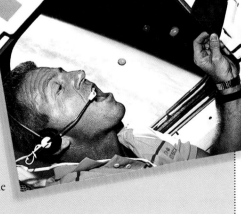

Visiting Other Worlds

I n the television series *Star Trek,* the crew of the starship *Enterprise* zoom through space at something called 'warp speed', a speed that's faster than light. For now, it is impossible to travel faster than light, which zips along at about 300,000 km (186,000 miles) per second. But who knows what the future will bring?

Because distances between objects in space are so great, if we want to do any serious space travelling we will have to figure out ways to propel ourselves faster. We also must become more self-sufficient so we don't have to carry so much food and water.

Just going to Mars would take roughly eight to nine months. That's a lot of meals, not to mention drinking and bathing water. And where would you put all the waste flushed down the toilet? Scientists are looking into self-contained environments for space travel. Everything would be recycled, including human waste and the carbon dioxide we exhale.

Would You Believe?

Bagging an Asteroid

I t's possible that **asteroids** could be a source of water for future space colonies. Some of these space rocks are up to 20 percent water. In one scenario *(above)*, cables grab an asteroid and hold it while a ship attaches a waterproof cone. Rocks scraped from the asteroid fill the cone. When the rocks are heated up the water will evaporate out of them. It can then be collected and stored.

Moon Base

A base on the Moon—it's not exactly the tropical paradise many people dream of, but it is the stuff of dreams. This NASA design shows an inflatable sphere where up to a dozen crew members could live. It is attached to another inflatable structure that serves as a landing facility. Astronauts landing on the Moon would hook up here and pass through to the habitation sphere. What would a Moon colony be used for? Probably either to mine the Moon's resources for use on Earth or as a launching place for deep-space missions.

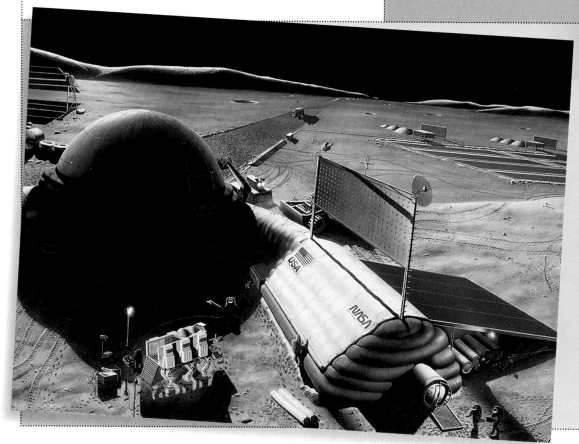

First Colony on a New World: Mars

When you step from your spaceship onto the red sands of Mars sometime in the next century, you'll be prepared for a challenging existence. You'll face temperatures as low as -123°C (-189°F), deadly radiation, and horrific dust storms. You will have brought everything you need to set up a colony, including recycling technology for oxygen, carbon dioxide, water, and solid waste. You will quickly set up greenhouses to grow fresh vegetables and fruit—luxuries even the fussiest children will crave after long months of travelling through space. And since you can't lug a lot of heavy building materials from Earth, for shelter you'll have to make do with what you have. The tipped-over shells of landing vehicles will be turned into living quarters, a clinic, and a lab. This painting gives you a sneak preview of what your new neighbourhood on Mars might look like. In the foreground, a landing craft with new pioneers parachutes to the surface.

How Long?

Martian Travelogue

In 1519, Portuguese explorer Ferdinand Magellan set sail to circumnavigate the globe and chart the great unknown. The fleet stayed away three long years. Most died of starvation and disease—including Magellan. Compared with that, a trip to Mars should seem a piece of cake. Scientists estimate that a modern-day Magellan could make the trip to Mars and back —with 20 days to explore—in about a year and a half. But Martian pioneers will have to contend with the effects of long stints in zero **gravity**—bone loss and muscle wasting—and the psychological effects of being cooped up in a spaceship for such a long time.

Imagine That!

In 1929, physicist J. D. Bernal proposed hollowing out an asteroid as an interstellar ark. The idea never got very far with aerospace experts. They pointed out that a ship made of rock would require unrealistic amounts of fuel to propel it through space. Such a rocky ship would be heavy, making it very slow—not a very realistic space vehicle! But it certainly intrigued science fiction writers, who have often used it in stories ever since.

Searching for Life

About 100 years ago, telescopes provided astronomers with their first really good look at the Red Planet—Mars. They were amazed by what appeared to be a network of structures. Were they canals, they wondered, dug by a Martian civilization as an irrigation system to bring water to dry fields? Decades later, however, their hopes were dashed when space probes sent back pictures of a desolate landscape with no signs of life. The only movement on the **planet** was from dust blown about by ferocious winds.

And yet, astronomers estimate that there are several hundred billion **stars** in our **galaxy.** Isn't it possible that at least one of them, besides Earth, has a planet with intelligent life? Some scientists believe searching for extraterrestrial life is a waste of time and money. Others think it's a noble exploration. What do you think?

Is There Life? Maybe So

What are the chances that there is life out there? Astronomer Frank Drake proposed this formula for figuring it out. However, it was meant more for discussion than to generate a real answer. Astronomers replace the letters with numbers. The numbers are not definite, so the answer, N, is not much better than a guess. What answer did Drake come up with? One hundred to 100 million civilizations might be out there.

Notes in a Bottle

Space probes launched from Earth may last for aeons. What are the chances some other civilization may bump into one, somewhere, someday? Why waste an opportunity! *Pioneer 10* and *Pioneer 11* each bear a plaque *(bottom)* engraved with the images of a man and a woman, and of the spacecraft itself. It also shows Earth's position within the **solar system** and the Milky Way, and relative to 14 **pulsars.** *Voyager 1* and *Voyager 2* carry videodisks *(centre)* with sights and sounds of Earth, including music, words, and even the songs of whales. The gold-plated cover *(top)* also shows Earth's position and explains how to play the disk. The symbol of two circles joined by a line on both messages is the molecular structure of hydrogen, the most common **element** in the universe.

$$N = R_* \; f_p \; n_e$$

N = number of civilizations in our galaxy willing and able to communicate. Based on this formula, some scientists figure between 100 and 100 million.

R_* **=** the probable rate of star births in our galaxy. Average number per year is 10. Life requires a home planet, which requires a star.

f_p **=** proportion of stars with planets **orbiting** around them. Astronomers assumed that planets form around all stars, setting f_p at 1.

n_e **=** percentage of planets with environments that can support life. Drake believed all solar systems could produce one, so he set this number at 1.

Radio Message to the Stars

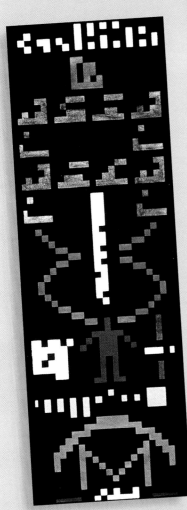

On and off since 1960, astronomers have tuned their radio telescopes *(lower right)* to frequencies they think aliens might use to communicate with others. Once or twice, they thought they had a fish on the line, but they were false alarms. Scientists face quite a challenge here. To capture an alien radio signal, a receiver will have to point in just the right direction and tune to just the right frequency—and there are billions of frequencies and billions of stars. In the meantime, scientists used the Arecibo telescope *(page 104)* in 1974 to send a radio message of their own. They sent it to M13, a star cluster in the **constellation** Hercules *(upper right),* because it has a lot of stars—about 100,000. The message used the binary system, which represents all numbers as groups of ones and zeros. Shown graphically at left, the message included information about humans

and about Earth's chemical composition. We'll have to wait awhile for an answer. Travelling at the speed of light *(page 10),* the message will take 24,000 years to get there. Any alien who receives it might need some time to come up with an answer, and then it will take another 24,000 years to make it back to Earth.

An exobiologist is a scientist who tries to answer questions about the possibility of life on other planets. Is there life out there? What kind of planet could support life? What other life forms are possible? Carl Sagan (1934-1996) was perhaps the world's most famous exobiologist. Although eager to find extraterrestrial life, Sagan took a scientific approach. When some scientists were convinced they saw vegetation on Mars, he supported the theory that what looked like vegetation was actually the darkening of the planet's surface by dust storms. He was right!

f_l = planets with life. Drake and colleagues felt that life arises fairly easily on habitable planets and so set this number at 1, too.

f_i = number of planets where intelligent life will evolve. Assuming a 1 in 10 chance, astronomers set this number at 0.1.

f_c = number of planets that have intelligent life able and willing to communicate. Assuming not all would, this number was set at 0.1.

L = life span of communicating civilizations. How long will such a civilization last, given disease and war? One thousand to one billion years.

Unusual Life Forms

Pressure Cooker

There is a moment of truth in every science fiction movie, when that alien first steps down from the spacecraft. Viewers hold their breath: what will the alien look like? Exobiologists—scientists exploring the possibility of life elsewhere in the universe—are less concerned with what aliens will look like than they are keenly interested in what the aliens will be made of and how they have adapted to conditions on their home world. Will they be carbon based, as all life on Earth is? Or will they be silica based, as some sci-fi writers have suggested? Will they photosynthesize? That is, will they transform their star's rays to make food the way plants on Earth use the Sun? Even the most hardened sceptics must agree that, if the day ever comes, there will be few events more exciting in human history than first contact with an alien.

Jupiter is a gas giant—a rocky **core** clad in layers of gas squeezed so tight by the planet's awesome gravitational pull that they have turned into a soupy mixture of solids and liquids. Near the surface of this gas soup, pressures are similar to those found deep under Earth's ocean—where strange (to humans, at least) life forms are able to exist.

Searing Heat

Temperatures on the surface of Venus reach a suffocating 500°C (900°F). Could anything survive on this fiery, barren world?

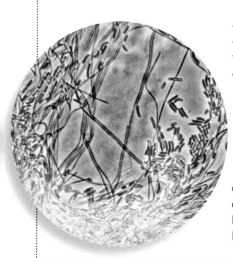

There are organisms on Earth that really like it hot. They're called thermophiles. The hot springs of Yellowstone National Park in the western United States are home to some of these heat lovers. Two species of bacteria, *Chloroflexus aurantiacus* and *Synechococcus lividus,* thrive in temperatures hot enough to boil fish, insects, crustaceans, and just about any other living thing. They probably couldn't quite survive the searing heat on Venus, but they certainly love a sizzling 70°C (160°F).

At 3,000 m (9,000 ft.) deep, the anglerfish *(above)* exists at unthinkable pressures in the pitch black of Earth's ocean. Its own glowing dorsal lure is the only light. Tiny deep-sea jellyfish *(right)* hover even deeper, as far as 3,800 m (12,500 ft.) below the surface.

Watery Realm

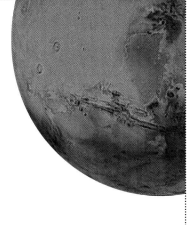

On Europa, Jupiter's smallest Galilean **moon,** a crust of ice covers what scientists believe is a deep ocean. At its bottom, geothermal vents might bubble chemicals into the water, supporting life forms similar to those living on the floor of some of Earth's deepest oceans.

Deep beneath the surface of Earth's ocean, far from sunlight, scientists have discovered new life forms. The creatures live around deep-sea vents, places on the ocean floor where hot, mineral-rich waters bubble up. Here, bacteria make food from chemicals in the water. They, in turn, are food for tiny crabs and giant tubeworms *(below).*

Freeze-Dried World

Astronomers know today that Mars is utterly arid and cold. Yet its surface shows the scars of erosion from aeons ago, when, scientists believe, Mars ran with the waters of 10,000 Amazon Rivers. Its **atmosphere** was thicker then, too. Some scientists think that Mars could have supported life, in those earlier, damper times. As the planet dried, could some life forms—perhaps microscopic ones—have adapted to the new environment? These scientists wonder whether, if they looked carefully, they might find fossil remains of former microscopic life in Martian rocks.

The tiny tardigrade (magnified 700 times, below) is about 85 percent water. If it has to, it can drop to as little as 2 percent, survive heat of 115°C (240°F) or equivalent cold, and later trot away unharmed. Perhaps something similar lives on Mars.

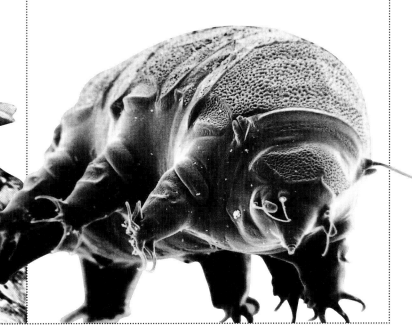

Picture Credits

Cover: book spine, Akira Fujii; front, Art by Jerry Lofaro; (inset) art by Stephen R. Wagner; NASA, photo no. 90-HC-515—The Studio of Wood Ronsaville Harlin, Inc.

All 'Fast Facts' icons by Jeff McKay.

Title page: Art by Stephen R. Wagner. Table of contents: Art by Jeff McKay—Anglo-Australian Observatory, photographed by David Malin —NASA; NASA/Jet Propulsion Laboratory, photo no. PIA01003—art by Jeff McKay; Jean-Loup Charmet, Paris. 6, 7: ©Frank Zullo/Photo Researchers. 8, 9: Space Telescope Science Institute (STScI); After de Lapparent, Geller and Huchra, 1986 *Astrophysical Journal Letters,* graphics by M. Kurtz ©1997, Smithsonian Astrophysical Observatory—art by Stephen R. Wagner. 10: Art by Jeff McKay (2)—Harvard College Observatory. 11: NASA/Johnson Space Center(JSC), Houston, Tex., photo no. STScI-973212-34—photo by Margaret Harwood, courtesy AIP Emilio Segrè Visual Archives; ©Jason Ware. 12, 13: Art by Stephen R. Wagner. 14: Roger Ressmeyer/©Corbis—art by Stephen R. Wagner; Robert P. Matthews. 15: NASA/Goddard Space Flight Center and the National Space Science Data Center—art by Jeff McKay—art by Stephen R. Wagner. 16: U.S. Department of Energy-Nevada Op/Corbis; ©Erich Schrempp/Photo Researchers; Robert Moss Photography, Alexandria, Va.; Pat O'Harva/Corbis; U.S. Army Night Vision Lab, Fort Belvoir, Va.; Robert Moss Photography, Alexandria, Va. (2)—art by Stephen R. Wagner. 17: ©NRAO/AUI—National Optical Astronomy Observatory (2)—Soft X-Ray Telescope, Lockheed-Martin Solar and Astrophysics Laboratory, on board *Yohkoh* satellite, ISAS, Japan; ©NRAO/AUI. 18: Courtesy The National Portrait Gallery, London—Einstein Archives, Hebrew University, Jerusalem; Jean-Loup Charmet, Paris—NASA/Johnson Space Center, photo no. 92-HC-644. 19: Art by Yvonne Gensurowsky, ©1991, Time-Life Books, Inc.—STScI, photo no. PRC95-43—art by Jeff McKay; Smithsonian Institution Archives (2). 20, 21: Art by Stephen R. Wagner; STScI, photo no. PR95-44a ; art by Stephen R. Wagner—art by Jeff McKay (2). 22, 23: Harvard College Observatory; Luke Dodd/Science Photo Library/Photo Researchers; (inset) Weldon Owen Pty. Limited; art by Jeff McKay (2). 24: Art by Rob Wood-Wood Ronsaville Harlin, Inc. 25: J. Morse/STScI and NASA, photo no. PRC95-24a—AIP Emilio Segrè Visual Archives, *Physics Today* Collection; ©1981, Anglo-Australian Observatory, photographed by David Malin—©1979 Anglo-Australian Observatory/Royal Observatory, Edinburgh, photographed by David Malin—copyright Anglo-Australian Telescope Board, photographed by David Malin— STScI, photo no. PR95-01a. 26, 27: STScI, photo no. PRC96-04; art by Don Davis, ©1985, Time-Life Books, Inc.—art by Stephen Bower of Bill Burrows and Associates, ©1988, Time-Life Books, Inc.; Roger Ressmeyer/©Corbis—courtesy Dr. Jocelyn Bell Burnell; UCO/Lick Observatory, photo no. U6(2). 28, 29: Ron Lussier; courtesy of Caltech/Palomar Observatory; Anglo-Australian Observatory, photographed by David Malin (2)—NASA, photo no. 90-HC-515; Roger Ressmeyer/©Corbis—David A. Harvey/©National Geographic Society—Joe Stancampiano/©National Geographic Society. 30: ©1995, Anglo-Australian Observatory, photographed by David Malin; ©1986, Anglo-Australian Observatory, photographed by David Malin—Anglo-Australian Observatory, photographed by David Malin—©1992, Anglo-Australian Observatory, photographed by David Malin—©1984, Anglo-Australian Observatory/ Royal Observatory Edinburgh, photographed by David Malin. 31: Allan Morton/Dennis Milon/Science Photo Library/Photo Researchers—Brad Whitmore, STScI/NASA, photo no. PRC97-34a; Hui Yang, University of Illinois and NASA, photo no. PRC96-27—Emmanuel Davoust, Observatoire Midi-Pyrénées. 32, 33: Scala, Florence; art by Fred Holtz— The British Library, London—©The Field Museum, Chicago, neg. no. A16231C, photographed by Ron Testa; art by Fred Holtz, ©1991, Time-Life Books, Inc.; George East/Science Photo Library/Photo Researchers —art by Jeff McKay—art by Fred Holz. 34: Roger Ressmeyer/Corbis-Bettmann—Corbis; art by Jeff McKay. 35: Art by Stephen R. Wagner, ©1991, Time-Life Books, Inc.; Scala, Florence—Royal Astronomical Society Library, London; Anglo-Australian Observatory, photographed by David Malin. 36: Scala, Florence—NASA/JPL/Cal Tech ©Science Graphics; art by Jeff McKay. 37: Art by Stephen R. Wagner, ©1991, Time-Life Books, Inc.; Corbis-Bettmann—Scala, Florence. 38: Scala, Florence; NASA/JPL/Cal Tech ©Science Graphics; art by Jeff McKay. 39: Corbis-Bettmann; art by Stephen R. Wagner ©1991, Time-Life Books, Inc.; Scala, Florence (2). 40: Scala, Florence; NASA/JPL/Cal Tech ©Science Graphics; art by Jeff McKay. 41: Scala, Florence; art by Stephen R. Wagner ©1991, Time-Life Books, Inc.—Scala, Florence. 42: NASA/JPL; David Miller. 43: Illustration by Lynette Cook, from *Discoveries: Stars and Planets*, Weldon Owen Pty. Ltd.—art by Stephen R. Wagner. 44, 45: Art by Don Davis, ©1985, Time-Life Books, Inc. (4)— ©Masanori Yamazaki, Gakken Co., Ltd. (2). 46, 47: Art by Damon Hertig, ©1990, Time-Life Books, Inc.—art by Stephen R. Wagner. 48, 49: Art by Jeff McKay; art by Maria DiLeo; art by Jeff McKay; Los Alamos National Laboratory; Yerkes Observatory Photograph—art by Rob Wood of Stansbury Ronsaville Wood, Inc., ©1985, Time-Life Books, Inc. 50: Giraudon; art by Alicia Freile (2)—art by Jeff McKay (2). 51: NASA; ©Association of Universities for Research in Astronomy Inc. (AURA), all rights reserved (2). 52, 53: The solar x-ray image is from the *Yohkoh* mission of ISAS, Japan. The x-ray telescope was prepared by the Lockheed-Martin Solar and Astrophysics Laboratory, the National Astronomical Observatory of Japan, and the University of Tokyo with the support of NASA and ISAS; High Altitude Observatory, Boulder, Colo. (3)—©Jack Finch/Science Photo Library/Photo Researchers. 54: Andrew W. Mellon Collection, National Gallery of Art, Washington, D.C.; art by Stephen R. Wagner.; NASA/National Space Science Data Center. 55: NASA/U.S. Geological Survey; art by Rob Wood of Stansbury Ronsaville Wood, Inc., ©1989, Time-Life Books, Inc.; art by Stephen R. Wagner—art by Rob Wood of Stansbury Ronsaville Wood, Inc., ©1989, Time- Life Books, Inc. 56, 57: From *The Secret Language of the Stars and Planets: A Visual Key to the Heavens*, by Geoffrey Cornelius and Paul Devereux, published by Chronicle Books, 1996; art by Stephen R. Wagner; painting ©1982, James Hervat—Sovfoto; NASA/Ames Research Center, Moffett Field, Calif.; NASA/JPL, photo no. P-45186— NASA/JPL, photo no. P-45389 —NASA/JPL, photo no. PIA 00089— NASA/JPL, photo no. PIA 00215. 58, 59: Photograph by Roderick Hook, courtesy of the Wheelwright Museum of the American Indian, no. P4,#4A; art by Stephen R. Wagner; art by Jeff McKay; digital image ©1996, Corbis, original image courtesy NASA; art by John Drummond —©Charlie Ott/Photo Researchers—art by Stephen R. Wagner. 60: Scala, Florence; art by Stephen R. Wagner; Alan Dyer—NASA, photo no. 90-HC-72—art by Stephen R. Wagner. 61: Lick Observatory, courtesy Pat Shand (7)—art by Jeff McKay (2)—Dennis di Cicco/Corbis; art by Stephen R. Wagner. 62, 63: NASA, photo no. S72-55417—NASA/JSC,

Houston, Tex.; NASA, photo no. 69-HC-687—NASA, photo no. S73-22871. 64: Mansell Collection, ©Time Inc. Picture Collection; art by Stephen R. Wagner; NASA/ USGS, photo no. PIA00407—NASA/ JPL—NASA/JPL, photo no. P-18635. 65: NASA/U.S. Geological Survey, photo no. PIA00300; NASA/JPL—art by Jeff McKay; NASA/ JPL, photo no. PIA01141. 66, 67: Barry Stauer for *People*—NASA, photo no. S94-32549 —NASA, photo no. 96-H-513; NASA/JPL, photo no. PIA01003; Lowell Observatory photograph (2)—Mary Evans Picture Library, London. 68: Scala, Florence/Musei Vaticani, Rome; art by Stephen R. Wagner; The Granger Collection, New York—art by Stephen R. Wagner. 69: NASA/U.S. Geological Survey, photo no. PIA00343. 70: Art by Jeff McKay; H. Himmel, MIT/NASA, photo no. PRC94-3. 71: NASA/JPL, photo no. PIA00065—Ludek Pesek/National Geographic Society. 72: NASA, photo no. P-217-60C—NASA/USGS, photo no. PIA00010. 73: NASA/JPL (2)—Paul M. Schenk, Lunar and Planetary Institute, Houston, Tex.—NASA/JPL; art by Jeff McKay. 74: Mary Evans Picture Library, London; art by Stephen R. Wagner; NASA/ USGS, photo no. PIA0040 —Ann Ronan Picture Library at Image Select, Harrow, Middlesex, England. 75: Art by Joe Bergeron, ©1990, Time-Life Books, Inc.—art by Jeff McKay. 76: NASA; art by Jeff McKay. 77: Art by Rick Sternback, ©1985 Time-Life Books, Inc.—Ann Ronan Picture Library, London; courtesy U.S. Naval Observatory, Washington, D.C., photographed by Larry Sherer. 78: NASA/JPL, photo no. PIA00733—NASA, photo no. PCP-23265C—NASA/USGS, photo no. PA00348—William H. Bond ©National Geographic Society. 79: Art by Rob Wood of Stansbury Ronsaville Wood, Inc., ©1990, Time-Life Books, Inc.; art by Jeff McKay. 80: Art by Michael Jaroszko; art by Stephen R. Wagner; NASA/University of Arizona, Erich Karkoschkas, photo no. PRC97-36A—USGS, Flagstaff, Ariz. 81: Corbis-Bettmann— art by Paul Hudson, ©1990 Time-Life Books, Inc.; art by Jeff McKay. 82: Victoria and Albert Picture Library, London; art by Stephen R. Wagner; NASA/JPL, photo no. PIA0046—Mary Lea Shane Archives of the Lick Observatory, University of California-Santa Cruz; Mary Evans Picture Library, London. 83: NASA, photo no. P-34764c—art by Ron Miller from *The Grand Tour*, ©1993, 1981 by Ron Miller and William K. Hartmann, used by permission of Workman Publishing Co., Inc., New York; art by Jeff McKay. 84: Palazzo Vecchio, Florence/The Bridgeman Art Library, London; art by Stephen R. Wagner; NASA/European Space Agency (ESA)/STScI; art by Paul Hudson, ©1990 Time-Life Books, Inc.; art by Jeff McKay—Lowell Observatory photograph— Weston & Son, Eastbourne, England, courtesy Mrs. Maxwell Phair/Ed Castle. 86: Art by Stephen R. Wagner; The Zinner Portrait Collection of San Diego State University-Special Collections; art by Rob Wood-Wood Ronsaville Harlin, Inc. (3). 87: Art by Stephen R. Wagner; from *The Little Prince*, by Antoine de Saint-Exupéry, ©1943 and renewed by Harcourt Brace & Co.; NASA, photo. no. PRP-43731. 88: Diebold-Schilling Chronik, 1513 ZB Luzern (Eigentum Korporation Luzern); art by Alfred T. Kamajian, ©1990, Time-Life Books, Inc.—Akira Fujii —courtesy The National Portrait Gallery, London. 89: ©Wally Pacholka; Jonathan Blair/National Geographic Image Collection. 90, 91: Art by Stephen R. Wagner; NASA/NSSDC, ESA Mission Giotto; art by Rob Wood-Wood Ronsaville Harlin, Inc., ©1990, Time-Life Books, Inc.—art by Jeff McKay. 92: Anthony Bannister, NHPA, Ardingly, Sussex, England; art by Stephen R. Wagner. 93: From *Between the Planets*, by Fletcher G. Watson, The Blackiston Company, Philadelphia, 1941— James M. Baker. 94: G. J. Wasserburg/Cal Tech and John DeVaney/ JPL; art by Rob Wood of Stansbury Ronsaville Wood, Inc., ©1990,

Time-Life Books, Inc. (4). 95: NASA, photo no. 76-HC-260—John Sanford/Science Photo Library/Photo Researchers, N.Y.—Illustration by James McKinnon from *The Nature Company Guide: Advanced Skywatching* ©Weldon Owen Pty. Ltd; Sovfoto. 96: Mary Evans Picture Library, London—The Metropolitan Museum of Art, Rogers Fund, 1948. (48.105.52); ©The British Museum, London. 97: The British Museum/Bridgeman Art Library, London; Reprinted from *Eyewitness Science: Astronomy*, courtesy DK Publishing, Inc.—Maryland Historical Society; Don Harris. 98, 99: ©Georg Gerster/Photo Researchers; courtesy English Heritage, London; Power Stock/Zefa, London— Macduff Everton/Corbis—Brian Vikander/Corbis; ©Solstice Project, photographed by Karl Kernberger—Robin Rector Krupp, Griffith Observatory. 100: Mary Evans Picture Library, London (2)—Corbis-Bettmann. 101: Jean-Loup Charmet, Paris; Fondation Saint-Thomas, Strasbourg—Smithsonian Institution Libraries/Charles H. Phillips— Scala, Florence. 102: Reprinted from *Eyewitness Science: Astronomy,* courtesy DK Publishing, Inc.; art by Jeff McKay (2); Yerkes Observatory photograph—©European Southern Observatory. 103: Royal Observatory, Edinburgh/Science Photo Library/Photo Researchers—art by Stephen R. Wagner, ©1990, Time-Life Books, Inc.—National Optical Astronomy Observatory. 104: David Parker, 1997/Science Photo Library/The Arecibo Observatory is part of the National Astronomy and Ionosphere Center, which is operated by Cornell University under a cooperative agreement with the National Science Foundation; Robert Frerck/Robert Harding Picture Library, London. 105: The Studio of Wood Ronsaville Harlin, Inc.; ©Dean Ellis/Ed Castle—courtesy NRAO/AUI (3). 106: The Studio of Wood Ronsaville Harlin, Inc.; Hui Yang, University of Illinois and NASA, photo no. PRC96-27 (2). 107: NASA, photo no. 61-48-001; S. Tererby, Extrasolar Research Corp. and NASA, photo no. PRc98-19. 108: NASA/JPL, photo no. P24653a—photo by Ruby Mera, UNICEF; USGS, Flagstaff, Ariz.—NASA/Ames Research Center, Moffett Field, Calif.—NASA, photo no. PIA00407—NASA, photo no.PIA00343— NASA, photo no. PIA00400—NASA/JPL, photo no. PIA00032— NASA/JPL, photo no. PIA00046. 109: NASA/JPL—art by Jeff McKay; NASA/USGS, photo no. PIA00407—European Space Agency; NASA/ JPL. 110: Jean-Loup Charmet, Paris (2). 111: Agence Ria-Novosti, Paris—Sovfoto (2); NASA, photo no. 61-MR2-26 and 69-HC-685. 112, 113: Mike Pattisall (notebook paper)—NASA, photo no. 96-Hc-657; NASA, photo no. S97-10538—art by Yvonne Gensurowsky of Stansbury Ronsaville Wood, Inc., ©1989, Time-Life Books, Inc.—NASA, photo no. S97-10538; NASA, photo no. 73-HC-470, 83-HC-428, and 92-HC-586. 114: Eagle Aerospace, Inc.; art by Stephen R. Wagner, ©1990, Time-Life Books, Inc. 115: Art by Rob Wood and Yvonne Gensurowsky of Stansbury Ronsaville Wood, Inc., based on original art by Carter Emmart, ©1989, Time-Life Books, Inc.—David A. Hardy/ Science Photo Library/Photo Researchers. 116: NASA/JPL, image no. p24652b and p24652a—NASA, photo no. 72-HC-133—art by Jeff McKay. 117: The Arecibo Observatory is part of the National Astronomy and Ionosphere Center, which is operated by Cornell University under a cooperative agreement with the National Science Foundation; courtesy Al Kelly—Joseph Sohm, Chromo Sohm Inc./Corbis—Cornell University —art by Jeff McKay. 118: NASA/Ames Research Center, Moffett Field, Calif.—courtesy Richard Castenholz; NASA/USGS, photo no. PIA00343 —Peter David/Planet Earth Pictures, London—Larry Martin/Planet Earth Pictures, London. 119: NASA/JPL; NASA/USGS, photo no. PIA00407—Woods Hole Oceanographic Institution; R. Shuster, Department of Entomology, University of California, Davis.

Glossary of Terms

Absolute brightness A measure of the actual rate of energy output of a star or other celestial object.

Absolute zero The point at which all molecules stop moving. In theory, it is the lowest possible temperature— 0° on the Kelvin temperature scale used in science and -273°C (-459°F).

Apparent brightness How bright a star or other astronomical object appears to a person on Earth. The apparent brightness depends on both the amount of energy being put out by the object and the object's distance from Earth.

Asteroid A small rocky body that orbits the Sun, ranging in size from dust particles to objects nearly 1,000 km (900 miles) across.

Asteroid belt A region of the solar system between the orbits of Mars and Jupiter where most asteroids are found.

Astronomical unit (AU) A unit of length equal to the distance between the Sun and the Earth —about 150 million km (93 million miles)—used to measure distances in the solar system.

Astronomy The scientific study of objects in space, including their size, composition, and motion.

Atmosphere The outermost gaseous layers of a planet, moon, or star. Some bodies have no atmosphere.

Atom The basic building block of the elements that make up all matter.

Axis An imaginary line through the poles of a celestial body around which the body spins.

Big Bang The moment, 13 to 15 billion years ago, when the universe began expanding from a tremendously dense speck.

Charged particles Basic units of atoms, such as protons and electrons, that have either a positive or a negative charge; they attract particles of opposite charge and repel particles with a like charge.

Comet A small body of ice and dust that orbits the Sun. When approaching the Sun, ice vapourizes into an envelope of dust and gas that forms a head and one or two tails.

Constellation A group of stars that forms a pattern in the sky; there are 88 named constellations.

Core The central region of a star, planet, or moon.

Corona (pl. **coronae**) The outermost layer of the Sun's atmosphere.

Cosmos Another word for the universe that comes from the Greek word *kosmos,* meaning 'world' or 'universe'.

Crater A circular, cup-shaped depression on the surface of a planetary body, usually caused by a meteorite impact.

Crust The solid surface layer of a moon or planet.

Density The amount of matter squeezed into a given amount of space; the more matter in this space, the greater the density.

Dust Small particles of matter, made mostly of silicates and carbon, that are mixed with gas in the vast space between the stars.

Eclipse An event that occurs when light from one celestial body is blocked as another body moves between it and the observer. During a **lunar eclipse** he Earth passes between the Moon and the Sun, darkening the Moon. During a **solar eclipse** the Moon passes between the Earth and the Sun, darkening the Sun.

Electromagnetic radiation Waves of energy that vary in length and move through space at the speed of light, 299,000 km (186,000 miles) per second.

Electromagnetic spectrum The range of electromagnetic radiation from long wavelength radio waves through microwaves, infrared rays, visible light, ultraviolet light, and x-rays to the shortest wavelength gamma rays.

Electron A negatively charged particle that normally orbits an atom's nucleus but may exist alone in isolation.

Element One of the more than 100 basic substances from which all other things are made. An element is formed of only one kind of atom.

Elliptical A shape resembling an elongated circle. Planets have elliptical orbits around the Sun.

Energy A measure of the ability of a body or system to do work or cause motion. There are various forms of energy, including heat, mechanical, electrical, nuclear, and radiant.

Galaxy A collection of stars that are held together by their own gravitational attraction; the smallest galaxies may contain a few million stars, whereas the largest may have a trillion stars.

Gas Matter in its most spread-out state, whereby it has neither a definite shape nor volume. Most gas in the universe is a form of hydrogen and accounts for a significant amount of a galaxy's mass.

Gravity The force responsible for the attraction of one object to another; the more mass an object has the greater its gravity.

Interplanetary medium The material between the planets in the solar system. It is composed of gas, dust, and electrically charged particles from the Sun.

Ion An atom that has lost or gained one or more electrons.

Kuiper belt A region of the solar system, beyond the orbit of Uranus, where large numbers of comets are thought to orbit.

Light-year A unit of length equal to the distance light travels through space in one year, about 10 trillion km (6 trillion miles).

Magnetic field lines Imaginary lines used to define the strength and position of a magnetic field. Lines of magnetic force tend to run from one magnetic pole to the other in the planets and the Sun.

Mantle The layer of a planet just below its crust.

Mass A measure of the total amount of matter an object contains.

Matter The substance or substances of which any physical object consists or of which it is composed.

Meteoroid A piece of rock or dust in space. Upon entering Earth's atmosphere they burn up in streaks of light called **meteors** hose that survive a passage through a planet's atmosphere and strike its surface are called **meteorites**

Moon A natural satellite of a planet, generally larger than 16 km (10 miles) in diameter; only Earth's moon is known as the Moon.

Nebula (pl. **nebulei**) A cloud of gas and dust found in the space between stars; often the birthplace of new stars or the remains of a dying star.

Neutron An uncharged particle that is found in the nucleus, or centre, of an atom.

Neutron star A star that has collapsed under gravity so much that it consists almost entirely of neutrons. They are also known as **pulsars.**

Nuclear fusion When two atomic nuclei, or centres of atoms, join together to form a heavier nucleus, releasing a lot of energy in the process; the source of power for the Sun and stars.

Nucleus (pl. **nuclei**) 1. The centre of an atom composed of protons and neutrons and orbited by electrons. 2. The ice-rock core of a comet.

Oort cloud A huge spherical region containing billions of comets thought to surround the solar system about one light-year from the Sun.

Orbit The path of an object that is revolving around another object.

Photons A packet of electromagnetic radiation that travels at the speed of light.

Planet A large body in orbit around the Sun or another star.

Plasma A gas-like substance made of charged particles, considered to be a fourth state of matter (along with gases, liquids, and solids). The Sun is mostly plasma.

Proton A positively charged particle found in the nucleus, or centre, of an atom.

Pulsar A spinning **neutron star** that gives off a beam of energy that sweeps past Earth each time the star rotates.

Quasar An extremely bright centre of a very distant galaxy; the most distant objects ever observed. The term quasar is shortened from 'quasi-stellar radio source'.

Radiation Energy that travels through space as waves. The light we see is one form of radiation.

Redshift The increase in the wavelength of electromagnetic radiation caused by an object in space moving away from an observer. For visible light, this means a shift toward the red end of the spectrum.

Reflecting telescope A telescope that uses mirrors to collect and focus light.

Refracting telescope A telescope that uses lenses to collect and focus light.

Revolution Moving in a curved path, or orbit, around a centre, such as the planets move around the Sun.

Rotation The spinning of a body, such as a planet, about an axis.

Satellite A celestial or man-made object in orbit around a larger object.

Solar system The Sun, planets, asteroids, comets, and other bodies that orbit the Sun; a star and the bodies in orbit around it.

Solar wind A stream of charged particles that flows out from the Sun and through the solar system.

Spectrograph An instrument that splits light or other electromagnetic radiation into its individual wavelengths, collectively known as a spectrum, and records the spectrum in a computer or as a photograph.

Spectrum The sequence of electromagnetic radiation arranged in order of wavelength, from long-wave radio waves to short-wave gamma rays. The most familiar example of a spectrum is a rainbow, which occurs when raindrops act as prisms to split sunlight into its component colours.

Star A luminous ball of gas that generates energy in its hot core by means of nuclear fusion. The Sun is a star.

Sunspot A dark patch on the Sun's surface that is cooler than the areas surrounding it. Sun-spots can be the size of Earth.

Supernova The explosion of an extremely massive star.

Tidal forces A gravitational pull exerted by an object in space whose strength or direction tends to alter the orbit or shape of another object.

Visible light That very tiny portion of the electromagnetic spectrum that human eyes see as light. It ranges from blue light, at the shorter wavelengths, to red light, at the longer wavelengths.

Wavelength The distance from crest to crest, or trough to trough, of an electromagnetic or other wave.

Index

Index

TIME-LIFE STUDENT LIBRARY
THE UNIVERSE

EDITOR: Jean Burke Crawford

Text Editor: Allan Fallow
Associate Editor/Research and Writing: Mary Saxton
Picture Associate: Lisa Groseclose
Picture Coordinator: Daryl Beard

Designed by: Jeff McKay and Phillip Unetic, 3r1 Group

Special Contributors: Joseph Alper, Patricia Daniels, Susan McGrath, Susan Perry
(text); Susan S. Blair, Patti Cass (research); Barbara Klein (index).
Senior Copyeditor: Judith Klein
Correspondents: Maria Vincenza Aloisi (Paris), Christine Hinze (London),
Christina Lieberman (New York).

ENGLISH EDITION

EDITOR: Mark Stephenson

Editorial: Kate Cann
Production: Justina Cox, Erika Dutting

Consultants:

Lee Ann Hennig teaches astronomy and is the planetarium director at Thomas
Jefferson High School for Science and Technology in Fairfax County, Virginia.
She has an undergraduate degree in astronomy and mathematics and a master's
degree in secondary science education with an emphasis in astronomy. She has
been a teacher since 1969 and has also been extremely active in astronomy
curriculum development at both the high-school and college levels. She serves
as an officer to a number of organizations that focus on astronomy education,
including the International Planetarium Society.

Steve Maran, the editor of *The Astronomy and Astrophysics Encyclopedia,* writes
widely on astronomy and is press officer for the American Astronomical Society.

Original US edition
©1997 Time Life Inc.

Authorized European English language edition
©1998 Time-Life Books B.V., Amsterdam

ISBN: 0 7054 3528 8

TIME-LIFE is a trademark of Time Warner Inc. U.S.A.
Printed by Toppan, Singapore

OTHER PUBLICATIONS INCLUDE

CHILDREN
A Child's First Library of Learning
Understanding Science & Nature

ADULT
What Life Was Like
Myth and Mankind
Lost Civilizations
Natural Ways to Health
The Art of Woodworking
Great Taste-Low Fat
Cookery Around the World
Mindpower

For information on and a full description of any of the Time-Life Books series
listed above, please call 0181 606 3100

1 2 3 4 5 6 7 8 9 10 11 12 13 14 15 16 17 18 19 20 21 22 23 24 25 26 27 28 29 30